Current
CONTROVERSIES

▌Homosexuality

Other Books in the Current Controversies Series

Homosexuality

Paul G. Connors, Book Editor

GREENHAVEN PRESS

An imprint of Thomson Gale, a part of The Thomson Corporation

Detroit • New York • San Francisco • New Haven, Conn. • Waterville, Maine • London

THOMSON

GALE

Christine Nasso, *Publisher*
Elizabeth Des Chenes, *Managing Editor*

For more information, contact:
Greenhaven Press
27500 Drake Rd.
Farmington Hills, MI 48331-3535
Or you can visit our Internet site at http://www.gale.com

ISBN-13: 978-0-7377-3721-9 (hardcover)
ISBN-10: 0-7377-3721-2 (hardcover)
ISBN-13: 978-0-7377-3722-6 (pbk.)
ISBN-10: 0-7377-3722-0 (pbk.)

Library of Congress Control Number: 2007934774

Contents

Chapter 1: What Are the Origins of Homosexuality?

Stefan Lovgren

A study measured the brain responses of homosexual and heterosexual men to the hormones present in male sweat. The findings revealed that the homosexual men's responses were similar to those of women, suggesting that brain activity and sexual orientation are linked.

Paul Varnell

Young homosexuals are attracted to *Batman* comics and project their early sexual feelings into the comics. However, millions of children and adolescents read *Batman* comics without developing any homosexual desires.

National Association for Research & Therapy of Homosexuality

Contrary to views expressed by gay activists and the mainstream media, there is no evidence to support the theory that homosexuality is genetic. In truth, scientific studies show that homosexuality results from an interaction of genes and environment.

Chapter 3: Should Society Encourage Increased Acceptance of Homosexuality?

Chapter 4: Should Government Sanction Gay and Lesbian Relationships?

No: Government Should Not Sanction Gay and Lesbian Relationships

Foreword

By definition, controversies are "discussions of questions in which opposing opinions clash" (Webster's Twentieth Century Dictionary Unabridged). Few would deny that controversies are a pervasive part of the human condition and exist on virtually every level of human enterprise. Controversies transpire between individuals and among groups, within nations and between nations. Controversies supply the grist necessary for progress by providing challenges and challengers to the status quo. They also create atmospheres where strife and warfare can flourish. A world without controversies would be a peaceful world; but it also would be, by and large, static and prosaic.

The Series' Purpose

The purpose of the Current Controversies series is to explore many of the social, political, and economic controversies dominating the national and international scenes today. Titles selected for inclusion in the series are highly focused and specific. For example, from the larger category of criminal justice, Current Controversies deals with specific topics such as police brutality, gun control, white collar crime, and others. The debates in Current Controversies also are presented in a useful, timeless fashion. Articles and book excerpts included in each title are selected if they contribute valuable, long-range ideas to the overall debate. And wherever possible, current information is enhanced with historical documents and other relevant materials. Thus, while individual titles are current in focus, every effort is made to ensure that they will not become quickly outdated. Books in the Current Controversies series will remain important resources for librarians, teachers, and students for many years.

In addition to keeping the titles focused and specific, great care is taken in the editorial format of each book in the series. Book introductions and chapter prefaces are offered to provide background material for readers. Chapters are organized around several key questions that are answered with diverse opinions representing all points on the political spectrum. Materials in each chapter include opinions in which authors clearly disagree as well as alternative opinions in which authors may agree on a broader issue but disagree on the possible solutions. In this way, the content of each volume in Current Controversies mirrors the mosaic of opinions encountered in society. Readers will quickly realize that there are many viable answers to these complex issues. By questioning each author's conclusions, students and casual readers can begin to develop the critical thinking skills so important to evaluating opinionated material.

Current Controversies is also ideal for controlled research. Each anthology in the series is composed of primary sources taken from a wide gamut of informational categories including periodicals, newspapers, books, U.S. and foreign government documents, and the publications of private and public organizations. Readers will find factual support for reports, debates, and research papers covering all areas of important issues. In addition, an annotated table of contents, an index, a book and periodical bibliography, and a list of organizations to contact are included in each book to expedite further research.

Perhaps more than ever before in history, people are confronted with diverse and contradictory information. During the Persian Gulf War, for example, the public was not only treated to minute-to-minute coverage of the war, it was also inundated with critiques of the coverage and countless analyses of the factors motivating U.S. involvement. Being able to sort through the plethora of opinions accompanying today's major issues, and to draw one's own conclusions, can be a complicated and frustrating struggle. It is the editors' hope that Current Controversies will help readers with this struggle.

Introduction

> *"To many heterosexual and homosexual admirers of Lincoln, his sexuality remains an enigma, and this mystery applies to homosexuality in general."*

For generations, writers have either inferred or claimed that President Abraham Lincoln was a homosexual. In 1926, the poet Carl Sandburg, in his best-selling biography of the sixteenth president, wrote that both Lincoln and his good friend Joshua Fry Speed maintained "a streak of lavender and spots soft as May violets." At the time "streak of lavender" was another way of saying that a male was a mama's boy; and afterward "lavender" became synonymous with homosexual. Although Sandburg did not describe the relationship between Lincoln and Speed in sexual terms, he obviously thought the relationship was peculiar. Sandburg based his belief on the fact that while in Springfield, Illinois, the twenty-eight-year-old Lincoln and the twenty-three-year-old merchant shared a double bed for four years. Though both men later married and had children, they remained close their entire lives. Speed later acknowledged, "no two men were ever so intimate."

Lincoln's sexuality continues to be of interest to writers and the general public because his actions seem so curious. For example, the historian Philip Nobile notes that as a boy, Lincoln wrote a poem about a boy marrying a boy and exhibited a lifetime preference for male company. As president, Lincoln shared a bed with his soldier-bodyguard in the summer White House in 1862. According to the regiment history, published three decades later, Captain David Derickson "advanced so far in the president's confidence and esteem that in Mrs. Lincoln's absence he frequently spent the night at his cottage, sleeping in the same bed with him, and—it is said—making use of his Excellency's night shirt!" Most recently, C. A. Tripp, a sex researcher and associate of Alfred Kinsey, founder of the Kinsey Institute for Research in Sex, Gender and Reproduction at Indiana University, wrote a controversial book called *The Intimate World of Abraham Lincoln*. In the book, which has received mixed reviews, Tripp argued that Lincoln had erotic and same-sex attractions throughout his life. He also had thorny relationships with nearly all the women in his life, including his wife Mary Todd Lincoln. The eminent historian David Herbert Donald, author of the acclaimed book *Lincoln*, rejects this thesis. He claims that there is no evidence that Lincoln was a homosexual; he raises the fact that Lincoln was married and fathered four children. Jean H. Baker, a biographer of Mrs. Lincoln, describes the relationship between the president and his wife as "bound together by three strong bonds, sex, parenting and politics." She discounts the charge that the Lincolns were not intimate with each other both on the grounds that it does not take into account the changing nature of marriage and courtship in the mid-nineteenth century and critiques the marriage using modern standards and sensibilities.

If Lincoln was gay, does it make any difference? Illinois state historian Thomas F. Schwartz believes that whether or not Lincoln desired or actually had sex with men has no bearing on the man who reconstructed the country, abolished slavery, and died a martyr's death. To Schwartz, the president's alleged homosexuality only matters if he made conscious decisions based on his sexuality, which then influenced his political behavior or public policy, which appears not to be the case. There is also the problem of what historians call "presentism," which interprets the past in terms of the present. As in the case of the Lincoln's marriage, it is difficult to apply modern ideological and political-identity notions of sexual orientation to the cultural climate of the mid-nineteenth century. There is no evidence that Lincoln thought of himself as a homosexual in the modern sense or defined himself by same-sex attractions or behavior. Therefore the question of whether Lincoln was gay is moot.

On the other hand, Lincoln's sexuality may have enormous symbolic significance. The writer Carol Lloyd argues that if Lincoln was gay, homophobic Republicans who both praise the founder of the Grand Old Party and denounce homosexuals would be forced to reexamine the deeper meaning of Lincoln's famous axiom, "With malice toward none; with charity for all." Certainly for queer theorists and gay scholars, the possibility of claiming the man who was one of America's greatest leaders as one of their own would provide the gay rights movement with a powerful symbolic champion.

To many heterosexual and homosexual admirers of Lincoln, his sexuality remains an enigma, and this mystery applies to homosexuality in general. In *Current Controversies: Homosexuality*, the authors spar over whether one's sexual orientation is genetic, behavioral, or even evolutionary. Writers question whether or not sexual identy can change through religious conversion and whether young homosexuals are attracted to the superhero *Batman*. In Chapters Two and Three, the writers offer their opinions on whether gays and lesbians face serious discrimination, and if society should encourage increased acceptance of homosexuality. Some authors are amazed how gays and lesbians can cry discrimination when their lifestyles are glamorized in popular culture and television, and are widely accepted by big business. The gay, lesbian, bisexual, and transgender community is equally perplexed about why their concerns are not taken seriously, primarily by devout Catholics and evangelical Protestants. The last chapter discusses the latest battle in the culture war: gay marriage. Interestingly enough, this issue even divides gays and lesbians. Like homosexuality itself, this is a complex issue with many cultural, legal, and political nuances. Though the country does not accept gays and lesbians on their own terms, the fact that many states and communities acknowledge domestic partnerships and civil unions and pass antidiscrimination laws against gays and lesbians is illustrative of how far the culture has shifted toward accepting our gay and lesbian brothers and sisters.

What Are the Origins of Homosexuality?

Chapter Preface

Alfred Kinsey is widely acknowledged as a major factor in changing attitudes about sex and homosexuality in the twentieth century. Both critics and admirers agree that he dramatically influenced the nature of sexual studies, forced a reexamination of public attitudes toward sex and sexuality, and challenged the medical and psychiatric establishments to reassess their views toward sexuality and homosexuality. Kinsey is credited with inspiring the feminist and gay and lesbian movements and thereby the sexual revolution of the 1960s. To appreciate why Kinsey is controversial, one has to realize that, prior to his controversial research in the 1950s, public discussions on sexuality were taboo and conventional thought held that most sexual activity occurred within the bounds of matrimony and within accepted moral standards. They believed homosexuality was a form of deviance practiced by only a small number of nonconformist men and women.

In 1947, Kinsey, a professor of entomology, founded the Institute for Research in Sex, Gender and Reproduction at Indiana University, now called the Kinsey Institute for Research, Sex, Gender and Reproduction. A year later, he published *Sexual Behavior in the Human Male*, followed by *Sexual Behavior in the Human Female* in 1953. More than 270,000 copies of the nearly 850-page book on female sexuality were sold in less than a month.

Kinsey considered himself an objective scientist. He thought human sexuality should be examined much the same way his fellow biologists and zoologists studied animal reproduction. In his above-mentioned publications, Kinsey had conducted sexual survey interviews with twenty thousand American men and women. The participants provided intimate information on how old they were when they first had sexual intercourse, number of sexual partners, frequency of premarital and extramarital sex, and incidence of homosexuality and lesbianism. Kinsey concluded that most sexual activity in America took place outside of marriage, was in the pursuit of sexual gratification, violated state and federal sex laws, and was a natural force that had been repressed, resulting in unfortunate consequences for individual happiness.

In regard to homosexuality, Kinsey believed that sexual behavior was properly understood both as physical contact and as psychic phenomena (desire, sexual attraction, and fantasy). From his research, he concluded that 10 percent of the population was homosexual and that sexuality was prone to change over time. In fact, he claimed that many homosexuals were once heterosexuals, who had undergone two or more such sexual orientation changes. In his 1948 report on male sexual behavior, Kinsey stated that almost 46 percent of the adult male subjects had "reacted" sexually to persons of both sexes, and 37 percent had at least one homosexual experience. The study also reported that 10 percent of American males surveyed were "more or less exclusively homosexual for at least three years between the ages of 16 and 55." In his study on female sexuality, the sex researcher reported that between 2 and 6 percent of females, aged 20–35 years of age, were more or less exclusively homosexual in experience.

The most controversial aspect of Kinsey's work was his research on child-adult sexual relationships gathered from pedophiles. Kinsey believed that very young children were capable of orgasms and that child-adult sexual contact was in itself not nearly so harmful as the shame induced by outraged adults. His most vocal critic is the author Dr. Judith A. Reisman, who charges that Kinsey based his research on a team of child molesters that violated over 2,000 children and infants. She also accuses the professor of sexually abusing at least 317 male children at his soundproof laboratory at Indiana University. In response, the Kinsey Institute director John Bancroft states that 1947 data on children in *Sexual Behavior of the Hu-*

man Male came from the journal of one adult pedophile. However, Bancroft did acknowledge that Kinsey granted the pedophile anonymity. He also claims that Kinsey never had sexual activity with children and interviewed children in the presence of their parents.

Sexuality May Be Biological

Stefan Lovgren

Stefan Lovgren reports for National Geographic News.

A new study [2005] shows that gay men respond differently from straight men when exposed to a suspected sexual stimulus found in male sweat.

When homosexual men smelled the odor of male sweat—more specifically, a chemical in the male hormone testosterone—their brains responded similarly to those of women.

The findings suggest that brain activity and sexual orientation are linked. It also supports an opinion held by most scientists, that people are born—not bred—gay.

"This is one more line of evidence that there's a biological substring for sexual orientation," said Dean Hamer, a geneticist at the National Institutes of Health [NIH] in Bethesda, Maryland.

Hamer is the author of *The Science of Desire: The Gay Gene and the Biology of Behavior*. He was not involved in the research, which was conducted by scientists at Karolinska Institute in Stockholm, Sweden.

The new study suggests that pheromones indeed play a part in making humans sexually attractive to one another.

The study was published today [May 10, 2005] in the research journal *Proceedings of the National Academy of Sciences*.

Reproductive Behavior

The scientists exposed heterosexual men and women and homosexual men to chemicals found in male and female sex hormones. One chemical is a testosterone derivative produced in men's sweat. The other chemical is an estrogen-like compound in women's urine.

These chemicals have long been suspected of being pheromones, molecules emitted by one individual that evoke some behavior in another of the same species. Pheromones trigger basic responses, such as sexual attraction, in many animals.

But scientists have long debated if humans respond to pheromones. The new study suggests that pheromones indeed play a part in making humans sexually attractive to one another.

In a previous study a few years ago, the Swedish researchers showed that the brain's hypothalamus region, which is involved in sexual behavior, becomes activated when men smell EST (the estrogen derivative) and women smell AND (the testosterone compound), but not vice versa.

A Study of Sexual Orientation

For their new study, the scientists added a sexual-orientation element, which revealed a difference in the brain activity of gay and straight men.

Gay men preferred odors from other gay men, while odors from gay men were the least preferred by straight men and women.

The researchers found that the testosterone compound activated the hypothalamus in homosexual men and heterosexual women, but not heterosexual men. Conversely, the estrogen compound activated the hypothalamus only in heterosexual men.

"It shows a different physiological response to the same external stimulus," said Ivanka Savic, a neuroscientist at the Karolinska Institute and the study's lead researcher. "This response [occurred] in the brain region involved in reproductive behavior."

When the study subjects sniffed scents such as cedar or lavender, all of their brains reacted only in the region that handles smells—not sexual behavior.

Biological Explanation

The results show that the human brain reacts differently to potential pheromones compared with common odors.

"It directly shows a link between brain activity and sexual orientation," said Hamer, the NIH geneticist.

Hamer cautions that the gay men's different brain activity could be either a cause of their sexual orientation or an effect of it. But, he said, "it certainly seems unlikely that somehow being interested in men would cause the brain to rewire itself in such a dramatic way."

Other studies have also found that gay and straight men respond differently to the body odors of others.

The new studies boost the hypothesis that homosexuality has a genetic basis and is not simply the result of learned behavior.

Scientists at the Monell Chemical Senses Center in Philadelphia, Pennsylvania, found that gay men preferred odors from other gay men, while odors from gay men were the least preferred by straight men and women.

Ongoing Studies

The Monell Center's results were released yesterday [May 9, 2005] and are to be published in the journal *Psychological Science* in September.

"There are many ongoing studies in the field, and I think that we soon will have better clarification," said Savic, the Karolinska Institute neuroscientist. "At the moment, there are no definite proofs."

However, the new studies boost the hypothesis that homosexuality has a genetic basis and is not simply the result of learned behavior.

"This, incidentally, is not in any way controversial for biologists," Hamer said. "It's completely expected from the basic tenets of biology. It's only controversial because of the social and political controversy over homosexuality."

Batman Comics Do Not Make Young Boys Gay

Paul Varnell

Paul Varnell writes a weekly column for the Chicago Free Press *and other gay newspapers.*

In the late 1940s and early 1950s critics of so-called "crime comic books" mounted a campaign against the conspicuous violence and brutality in many comics which the critics charged could and did lead impressionable young people to engage in violent and criminal behavior.

The most comprehensive attack was a widely discussed 1954 book called *Seduction of the Innocent* by Dr. Fredric Wertham, a senior psychiatrist for the New York City Department of Hospitals and director of mental hygiene clinics at Bellevue Hospital.

I once read that Wertham also claimed that some comic books promoted homosexuality so I wondered what Wertham said. Not a lot, it turned out. His 400 page book devoted only six pages to homosexuality, primarily in what he called "the Batman type of story." But what he said was interesting.

Batman Promotes Unconscious Homosexual Fantasies?

Wertham does not claim that Batman and Robin are homosexual, but that "the Batman type of story"—meaning an adult plus youth crime fighting team—could stimulate "children" to have homosexual fantasies without realizing it, and could reinforce homosexual fantasies in adolescents who have already developed homosexual feelings.

Wertham's discussion is not very clearly organized, but drawing on popular stereotypes about homosexuals and then-

"Batman—Gay Recruiter?" *Chicago Free Press*, June 8, 2005. Reproduced by permission.

prevalent theories of sexual psychopathology, he points to four aspects of the *Batman* comics to support his claim.

Wertham had no trouble finding homosexuals—in therapy, of course—who said they had read Batman *comic books and counted them among their favorite readings.*

First, there is the paederastic structure, if not content, of Batman and Robin's relationship. "The Batman type of story helps to fixate homoerotic tendencies by suggesting the form of an adolescent-with-adult or Ganymede-Zeus type of love-relationship."

Second, Batman and Robin live in a suspiciously elegant, dandified home. "At home they lead an idyllic life. They are Bruce Wayne and 'Dick' Grayson. They live in sumptuous quarters, with beautiful flowers in large vases, and have a butler, Alfred. Batman is sometimes shown in a dressing gown. . . . It is like a wish dream of two homosexuals living together." So Noel Coward [a gay English playwright who lived a glamorous lifestyle]!

It is worth noticing that Wertham has to reverse the usual structure of his argument here. In crime comics, it is the criminals who are fascinating and likely to be imitated. But in the *Batman* comics it is the heroes who are attractive—far too much so—and likely to be imitated.

Third, Wertham's sharp eye detects ostentatious genital display. Batman is an example of "the muscular male super-type, whose primary sex characteristics are usually well-emphasized." As for Robin, he is "a handsome ephebic boy, . . . usually shown in his uniform with bare legs. He often stands with his legs spread, the genital region discreetly evident."

Fourth, just as homosexuals were thought to hate women, Wertham views Batman as "anti-feminine." There are only "masculine, bad, witchlike or violent women" he says, and "if the girl is good looking she is undoubtedly the villainess. If she is after Bruce Wayne, she will have no chance against Dick." Wertham seems to intend the snickering joke.

Young Homosexuals
Are Attracted to Batman

Wertham had no trouble finding homosexuals—in therapy, of course—who said they had read *Batman* comic books and counted them among their favorite reading. And for Wertham that seems to close the case. But Wertham's argument runs into two crippling objections.

Young homosexuals would be attracted to Batman *comics and project their early, perhaps inchoate sexual feelings into the comics while young heterosexuals simply do not.*

Most obviously, millions of children and adolescents read *Batman* comic books without feeling or developing any homosexual fantasies or desires, yet Wertham offers no theory about why the homosexually "seductive" comics had absolutely no impact on the vast majority of readers.

Then too, although Wertham lays stress on the idea that the comics "seductively" can arouse unconscious homosexual fantasies, the evidence he offers contradicts that. All of the young homosexuals he discusses seem to have been aware at an early age that they were in some way or other attracted to men.

So Wertham has the causation backwards. The simplest explanation is that far from the "Batman type of story" being able to make some young men homosexual, young homosexuals would be attracted to *Batman* comics and project their early, perhaps inchoate sexual feelings into the comics while young heterosexuals simply do not. End of story.

There was no need to postulate mysterious psychiatric mechanisms such as "unconscious" homosexual fantasies and "fixated" homosexual "patterns" and no evidence that such things even existed.

The Reappearance of Alfred the Butler

In response to the widespread criticism and threats of legislative action, the violence and horror comic books were significantly toned down and criticism of those abated. But the suggestion that Batman's household had a homoerotic character continued to shadow the series.

Finally, in 1964, *Batman* editor Julius Schwartz decided to try to scotch the rumors once and for all by getting rid of the faithful butler Alfred Pennyworth.

According to Mark Cozza Vaz's history of *Batman* comics, *Tales of the Dark Knight*, Schwartz recalled: "Many people were questioning why three males were living together. So I said, 'Okay, I'll kill off one of the males and put a woman in there!' And the woman turned out to be Aunt Harriet, the aunt of Dick Grayson. . . . I guess that was pretty drastic, killing off Alfred."

But happily within just a few years the *Batman* television program decided that it wanted to include Alfred, so Alfred was duly revived from the dead, once again to serve the original ambiguously non-gay duo.

There Is No Evidence that Homosexuality Is Genetic

National Association for Research & Therapy of Homosexuality

The National Association for Research & Therapy of Homosexuality (NARTH) is a nonprofit, education organization dedicated to affirming a complementary male-female model of gender and sexuality.

Many laymen now believe that homosexuality is part of *who a person really is* from the moment of conception.

The "genetic and unchangeable" theory has been actively promoted by gay activists and the popular media. Is homosexuality really an inborn and normal variant of human nature?

No. There is no evidence that shows that homosexuality is simply "genetic." *And none of the research claims there is.* Only the press and certain researchers do, when speaking in sound bites to the public.

Mainstream Media Misled Public

In July of 1993, the prestigious research journal *Science* published a study by Dean Hamer which claims that there might be a gene for homosexuality. Research seemed to be on the verge of proving that homosexuality is innate, genetic and therefore unchangeable normal variant of human nature.

Soon afterward, National Public Radio trumpeted those findings. *Newsweek* ran the cover story, "Gay Gene?" The *Wall Street Journal* announced, "Research Points Toward a Gay Gene . . . Normal Variation."

National Association for Research & Therapy of Homosexuality, "Is There a 'Gay Gene'?" www.narth.com, September 21, 2004. Reproduced by permission.

Of course, certain necessary qualifiers were added within those news stories. But only an expert knew what those qualifiers meant. The vast majority of readers were urged to believe that homosexuals had been proven to be "born that way."

In order to grasp what is *really* going on, one needs to understand some little-known facts about behavioral genetics.

Linkage Studies

Dean Hamer and his colleagues had performed a common type of behavioral genetics investigation called the "linkage study." Researchers identify a behavioral trait that runs in a family, and then:

1. look for a chromosomal variant in the genetic material of that family, and

2. determine whether that variant is more frequent in family members who share the particular trait.

To the layman, the "correlation" of a genetic structure with a behavioral trait means that trait "is genetic"—in other words, *inherited.*

In fact, it means absolutely nothing of the sort, and it should be emphasized that there is virtually no human trait without innumerable such correlations.

We think that the data in fact provide strong evidence for the influence of the environment.

But before we consider the specifics, here is what serious scientists think about recent genetics-of-behavior research. From *Science*, 1994:

Time and time again, scientists have claimed that particular genes or chromosomal regions are associated with behavioral traits, only to withdraw their findings when they were not replicated. "Unfortunately," says Yale's [Dr. Joel] Gelernter, "it's hard to come up with many" findings linking spe-

cific genes to complex human behaviors that have been replicated. ". . . All were announced with great fanfare; all were
greeted unskeptically in the popular press; all are now in
disrepute."

Environment Is an Important Factor

Two American activists recently published studies showing
that if one of a pair of identical twins is homosexual, the
other member of the pair will be, too, in just under 50% of
the cases. On this basis, they claim that "homosexuality is genetic."

But two other genetic researchers—one heads one of the
largest genetics departments in the country, the other is at
Harvard—comment:

> While the authors interpreted their findings as evidence for
> a genetic basis for homosexuality, we think that the data in
> fact provide strong evidence for the influence of the envi-
> ronment.

---

*Researchers' public statements to the press are often grand
and far-reaching. But when answering the scientific community, they speak much more cautiously.*

The author of the lead article on genes and behavior in a
special issue of *Science* speaks of the renewed scientific recognition of the importance of environment. He notes the growing understanding that:

> . . . the interaction of genes and environment is much more
> complicated than the simple "violence genes" and "intelli-
> gence genes" touted in the popular press. The same data
> that show the effects of genes, also point to the enormous
> influence of nongenetic factors.

Media Offers Partial Truths

Researchers' public statements to the press are often grand
and far-reaching. But when answering the scientific community, they speak much more cautiously.

"Gay gene" researcher Dean Hamer was asked by *Scientific American* if homosexuality was rooted solely in biology. He replied:

> "Absolutely not. From twin studies, we already know that half or more of the variability in sexual orientation is *not inherited*. Our studies try to pinpoint the genetic factors . . . not negate the psychosocial factors."

But in qualifying their findings, researchers often use language that will surely evade general understanding making statements that will continue to be avoided by the popular press, such as:

> . . . the question of the appropriate significance level to apply to a nonMendelian trait such as sexual orientation is problematic.

Sounds too complex to bother translating? This is actually a very important statement. In layman's terms, this means:

It is *not possible* to know what the findings mean—*if anything*—since sexual orientation cannot possibly be inherited in the direct way eye color is.

Thus, to their fellow scientists, the researchers have been honestly acknowledging the limitations of their research. However, *the media doesn't understand that message*. Columnist Ann Landers, for example, tells her readers that "homosexuals are born, not made." The media offers partial truths because the scientific reality is simply too unexciting to make the evening news; too complex for mass consumption; and furthermore, not fully and accurately understood by reporters.

There are no "lite," soundbite versions of behavioral genetics that are not fundamentally in error in one way or another.

Nonetheless, if one grasps at least some of the basics, in simple form, it will be possible to see exactly why the current research into homosexuality means so little and will continue to mean little, even should the quality of the research methods improve so long as it remains driven by political, rather than scientific objectives.

Seeing Through the Distortion

There are only two major principles that need to be carefully understood in order to see through the distortions of the recent research. They are as follows:

1. *Heritable* does not mean *inherited*.

2. Genetics research which is truly meaningful will identify, and then focus on, only traits that *are directly inherited*.

Almost every human characteristic is in significant measure *heritable*. But few human behavioral traits are directly *inherited*, in the manner of height, for example, or eye color. *Inherited* means "directly determined by genes," with little or no way of preventing or modifying the trait through a change in the environment.

Suppose you are motivated to demonstrate—for political reasons—that there is a basketball gene that *makes* people grow up to be basketball players. You would use the same methods that have been used with homosexuality: (1) twin studies; (2) brain dissections; (3) gene "linkage" studies.

What the majority of respected scientists now believe is that homosexuality is attributable to a combination of psychological, social, and biological factors.

The basic idea in twin studies is to show that the more genetically similar two people are, the more likely it is that they will share the trait you are studying.

So you identify groups of twins in which *at least one* is a basketball player. You will probably find that if one identical twin is a basketball player, his twin brother is *statistically more likely* be one, too. You would need to create groups of different kinds of pairs to make further comparisons—one set of identical twin pairs, one set of nonidentical twin pairs, one set of sibling pairs, etc.

Using the "concordance rate" (the percentage of pairs in which *both* twins are basketball players, or *both* are not), you would calculate a "heritability" rate. The concordance rate would be quite high—just as in the concordance rate for homosexuality.

Then, you announce to the reporter from *Sports Illustrated*: "Our research demonstrates that basketball playing is strongly heritable." (And you would be right. It would be "heritable"—but not directly inherited. Few readers would be aware of the distinction, however.)

Soon after, the article appears. It says:

> ... New research shows that basketball playing is probably *inherited*. Basketball players are apparently "born that way!" A number of outside researchers examined the work and found it substantially accurate and well performed ...

But no one (other than the serious scientist) *notices* the media's inaccurate reporting.

Scientists Often Don't Tell the Truth

Then you move on to conduct some brain research. As in the well-known LeVay brain study which measured parts of the hypothalamus, your colleagues perform a series of autopsies on the brains of some dead people who, they have reason to believe, were basketball players.

Next, they do the same with a group of dead nonbasketball players. Your colleagues report that, on average, "Certain parts of the brain long thought to be involved with basketball playing are much larger in the group of basketball players."

A few national newspapers pick up on the story and editorialize, "*Clearly, basketball playing is not a choice. Not only does basketball playing run in families, but even these people's brains* are different."

You, of course, as a scientist, are well aware that the brain changes with use ... indeed quite dramatically. Those parts responsible for an activity get larger over time, and there are specific parts of the brain that are more utilized in basketball playing.

Now, as a scientist, you will not *lie* about this fact, *if asked* (since you will not be), but neither will you go out of your way to offer the truth. The truth, after all, would put an end to the worldwide media blitz accompanying the announcement of your findings.

Now, for the last phase, you find a small number of families of basketball players and compare them to some families of nonplayers. You have a hunch that of the innumerable genes likely to be associated with basketball playing (those for height, athleticism, and quick reflexes, for example), some will be located on the x-chromosome.

There is no evidence that homosexuality is simply "genetic"—and none of the research itself claims there is.

You won't say these genes *cause* basketball playing because such a claim would be scientifically insupportable, but the public thinks "caused by" and "associated with" are synonymous.

After a few false starts, sure enough, you find what you are looking for: among the basketball-playing families, one particular cluster of genes is found more commonly.

Homosexuality Is Attributable to Many Factors

Now, it happens that you have some sympathizers at National [Public] Radio, and they were long ago quietly informed of your research. They want people to come around to certain beliefs, too. So, as soon as your work hits the press, they are on the air: "*Researchers are hot on the trail of the Basketball Gene. In an article to be published tomorrow in *Sports Science* . . ."

Commentators pontificate about the enormous public-policy implications of this superb piece of science. Two weeks later, there it is again, on the cover of the major national newsweekly: "Basketball Gene?"

Now what is wrong with this scenario? It is simple: of course basketball playing is associated with certain genes; of course it is *heritable*. But it is those intermediate physiological traits—muscle strength, speed, agility, reflex speed, height, etc.—which are themselves directly *inherited*. Those are the traits that make it likely one will be *able* to, and will *want* to, play basketball.

In the case of homosexuality, the inherited traits that are more common among male homosexuals might include a greater than average tendency to anxiety, shyness, sensitivity, intelligence, and aesthetic abilities. But this is speculation. To date, researchers have not yet sought to identify these factors with scientific rigor.

What the majority of respected scientists now believe is that homosexuality is attributable to a combination of *psychological, social, and biological factors*.

From the American Psychological Association:

"[M]any scientists share the view that sexual orientation is shaped for most people at an early age through complex interactions of biological, psychological and social factors."

From "Gay Brain" Researcher Simon LeVay:

"At this point, the most widely held opinion [on causation of homosexuality] is that *multiple factors* play a role."

From Dennis McFadden, University of Texas neuroscientist:

"Any human behavior is going to be the result of *complex intermingling of genetics and environment*. It would be *astonishing* if it were not true for homosexuality."

From Sociologist Steven Goldberg:

"*I know of no one* in the field who argues that homosexuality can be explained without reference to environment factors."

As we have seen, there is no evidence that homosexuality is simply "genetic"—*and none of the research itself claims there is.*

Only the press and certain researchers do, when speaking in sound bites to the public.

Male Homosexuality
Is a Result of Evolution
and Social Factors

Pieter R. Adriaens and Andreas De Block

Pieter R. Adriaens is on the faculty of the Institute of Philosophy, University of Leuven, Belgium, and Andreas De Block is on the faculty of philosophy at Radboud University, Nijmegen, The Netherlands.

Nearly all evolutionary accounts of (human) homosexuality assume that homosexuals do not reproduce, or at least that they do so considerably less than heterosexuals. Despite their own frequent exhortations that one should not consider the behavioral patterns of current homosexuals to be the only possible kind of same-sex sexuality, few, if any, evolutionary theorists have actually reviewed the history of homosexuality. Instead, they have assumed that data about the reproduction of contemporary North American and European homosexuals are representatives of the entire evolutionary history of homosexuality. It may be true that *contemporary* homosexuals have only one fifth (up to one tenth) as many children as contemporary heterosexuals, but there is no compelling reason to think that this has always been the case. One of the more surprising findings of recent historical and anthropological research on homosexuality is that most men who engaged in same-sex sexual practices simultaneously married. Thus they had sexual relationships with men (mostly boys or adolescents) and with women.

Pieter R. Adriaens and Andreas De Block, "The Evolution of a Social Construction: The Case of Male Homosexuality," *Perspectives in Biology and Medicine*, vol. 49, no. 4, autumn 2006, pp. 573–576, 580–583. Copyright © 2006 The Johns Hopkins University Press. Reproduced by permission.

Historically Most Homosexuals Were Married

As strange as the idea of a homosexual marrying a woman may seem to some of us today, such marriages not only occurred frequently in many ancient societies, they continue to occur in many contemporary ones, including the United States. Two examples illustrate this point. In Japan today, marriageable women often read gay magazines because they contain personal ads from homosexuals whose families and employer are urging them to marry and beget children: "So long as those obligations [marriage and parenthood] are met, one's sexual activity is not anyone else's legitimate concern." And in ancient Greece, Spartan boys (*eromenoi*) were drilled under the eagle's eye of their older lovers, the *erastai*, so as to become good warriors. Spartan soldiers are said to have sacrificed to Eros before entering the battlefield, in the belief that their fate was closely tied to the intimate relationship they had with their fellow warriors. Most of the boys married, however, which amounted to having intercourse with their wives at least once a month. The remaining nights they spent with their *erastes* (who often acted as the newlyweds' Maecenas for some time after the marriage) or with their own *eromenos*. Indeed, only the *eromenoi* who married and raised children were allowed to become *erastai* themselves: "Exclusive pederasty [intimate relations between men and adolescent boys] was negatively sanctioned, but pederasty was expected."

Historical changes in 18th-century politics, science, and philosophy led to the construction of a homosexual identity.

In short, an abundance of historical and anthropological evidence suggests that male same-sex sexuality frequently involved, and still involves, married men. For the majority of men engaging in same-sex sexual activities, such activities have always been complementary to, and not a replacement of marital sexuality. Only recently has homosexuality been redefined as *exclusive* sexual activity with others of the same sex, which necessarily forecloses the biological possibility of having children. Today (some) male homosexuals have sex only with men, and never with women, but such exclusivity is by no means representative of the history of same-sex sexuality.

Exclusive Same-Sex Sexuality

Homosexuality as we now know it is definitely a social construction. In Western Europe, the era of exclusive same-sex sexuality probably began in the early 18th century. [Historian Randolph] Trumbach, for example, has argued that before about 1700, many English men maintained sexual relationships with women as well as with younger boys: "homosexual activity occurred between most men and boys. . . . Sodomy was therefore so widespread as to be universal. But it was always structured by age. . . ." While the religious authorities disapproved of this custom, public opinion saw nothing wrong with it, provided the older lover played the active part. But around 1700, a major shift in sexual morays started to set in: older men, who were called (and called themselves) *mollies* or *sodomites*, shifted roles and began playing the passive part that had, traditionally, been reserved for the adolescent. Moreover, some mollies and sodomites now desired *only* men: they neither married nor raised children. Such exclusive sexual preference, however, is just one of the characteristics of this "wholly new" kind of same-sex sexuality. Modern homosexual partners also lack significant status differences, and they identify themselves with a gender that combines characteristics of both femininity and masculinity. These three characteristics, exclusivity, equality, and self-identification—and certainly their combination—are quite new in the history of human same-sex sexuality.

[Michel] Foucault [the French philosopher and historian], has tried to explain the genesis of this exclusive kind of same-sex sexuality. According to him, historical changes in 18th-century politics, science, and philosophy led to the construction of a homosexual identity. Around 1700, authorities came to see the control of sexuality as an instrument with which to reach their goals of economic efficiency and political conservatism. The sciences developed "discourses" to control sexuality, and these in turn gave rise to the medicalization of sexuality in general and of homosexuality in particular. Sodomy was well known, but it had, until then, been a purely legal issue, much like adultery. From the 18th century on, homosexuality became not only illegal, but also "unnatural": it became an illness. And that is just the beginning. Prior to this medicalization, homosexuality was not a matter of identity but a matter of preference. These preferences could change during an individual's life, and they usually did not lead to exclusivity. The medicalization of same-sex sexual behavior changed all this. It transformed sexual preferences into decisive determinants of people's identities. "I am a homosexual" suddenly became an acceptable answer to the question "What are you?" While the sodomite prior to 1700 had been at most an outlaw, from 1700 on the homosexual became a member of a kind, or even a species. People might change what they like, but it is much more difficult to change what they are.

Exclusive Homosexuals or Heterosexuals

The authorities invented "the homosexual" with the help of such seemingly objective sciences as sexology and psychiatry. This invention was also a creation. Once the homosexual identity had been constructed, most people tailored their behavior to one of the two "basic" categories, homosexual or heterosexual: they became exclusive homosexuals or exclusive heterosexuals. In other words, while these sciences pretended to explain a reality, they actually changed that reality: scientists shaped stories, and these stories shaped people. Talking about refugee women in Canada, for example, [philosopher Ian] Hacking says that "in consequence of being so classified, individual women and their experiences of themselves are changed by being so classified." Exactly the same might be said about male homosexuals, whether in the 18th century or in contemporary societies. Hacking would say that both "refugee women" and "homosexuality" are interactive kinds, as opposed to natural kinds.

Homosexuality may be a relatively recent social construction, . . . but same-sex sexual behavior has been going on for millions of years.

Foucault's historical nominalism with regard to homosexuality is as baffling as it is convincing, but it harbors enormous critical potential for scientific approaches to sexuality, as it sheds a whole new light on biological theories of homosexuality. Whereas most evolutionary psychologists consider homosexuality to have some kind of natural essence, Foucault suggests it is actually an 18th-century social construction. Some radical social constructivists have even gone one step further and proclaimed that Foucault's account must jeopardize any so-called naturalistic account of homosexuality, but this radical conviction is rooted in the assumption that every scientific explanation is profoundly essentialist, an assumption—as we will show—that is untenable. Homosexuality may be a relatively recent social construction, and thus an evolutionary oddity, but same-sex sexual behavior has been going on for millions of years, a fact suggested by the abundant evidence of instances of this behavior in the animal world. . . .

Social Factors in Homosexual Identity

The first thing that has to be explained is the 18th-century transition from a longstanding behavioral pattern—occasional same-sex sexual behavior—to a radically new invention, the homosexual identity. Whence this new identity? Foucault attributes the creation of the so-called "third gender" to the rise of new sciences such as psychiatry and sexology. To establish their own power and authority, psychiatrists, doctors, and sexologists joined in the social establishment's wish to control sexuality and to turn it into something economically useful and politically conservative.

While Foucault is right in saying that these forces played a key role in the creation of the homosexual identity, other factors may also have been important. The 18th century heralded the industrial revolution, stimulating the expansion of big cities, where it became increasingly more difficult to maintain family alliances. The collapse of the traditional family was indeed one of the preconditions for the development and dissemination of a new, modern kind of homosexuality. [Author Stephan] Murray writes that it is "the availability of social insurance other than family support and of sufficient housing stock (at least some of which families do not control) that make possible the formation of a critical mass of those desiring and/or having same-sex relationships." As well, the increasing population density defined sharper hierarchies. These changes necessitated the formation of alliances with non-kin and may have triggered adaptive strategies such as same-sex sexual behavior. The lack of social coherence may have intensified this form of sexual behavior, which gradually paved the way for the formation of a more exclusive kind of same-sex sexuality—a transition that may have played an important role in the establishment's anti-homosexual reaction. It is perhaps no wonder that, historically, the first real homosexual subcultures are to be found in big cities such as 18th-century London. . . .

The Rise of Homophobia

Foucault claims that homophobia is due to the decline of the *amicitia,* a particular, affective kind of friendship between males that often included same-sex sexual behavior: "Once friendship had disappeared as a culturally accepted relationship, the question was raised: 'But what are these men doing together?' At that moment, the problem [of homophobia] made its first appearance." Sexual contact between males was seen as some sort of plot, and the inability to understand it made the public at large fearful and caused them to repudiate it. To avert the fear, Foucault contends, these men were tagged with a new identity based on their sexual activities: the homosexual identity. Indeed, the construction of the homosexual identity resulted from the fact that same-sex sexual behavior was suddenly seen as subversive and repugnant. Same-sex sexuality simply did not fit in with the then prevailing Cartesian view of man and world, Foucault says, so people tried to control and oppress it by constructing a category for it.

People adopt the homosexual identity because they are cultural beings.

Foucault's argument assumes that whatever we do not understand only gains our fear and repudiation. However, the question remains why such repudiation—resulting in this case, in homophobia—occurred so suddenly at the beginning of the 18th century. Foucault's allegation that same-sex sexual behavior only became a problem in the 18th century is a gross historical error. Same-sex sexual behavior had by then been commonplace for hundreds of years, and that in spite of a fierce inquisition that had first reared its head in the 13th century. Exclusive homosexuality may be an 18th-century social construction, but homophobia is not. In fact it seems that (passive) homosexuals have never been accepted in Western culture. Pre-Christian Roman law stipulated that passivity in a same-sex sexual relationship should entail a loss of civic rights. And Biblical law was also not kindly disposed towards homosexuals, whether passive or active. Its contempt for the "sin of sodomy" resulted in a horrendous hunt for homosexuals throughout more than 14 centuries.

The question is not why there is such a sudden occurence of homophobia around 1700, but rather why same-sex sexual behavior has so consistently, and with ever-increasing vehemence since the rise of Christianity, been regarded as subversive.... The sudden rise of homophobia around 1700 is probably due to a feedback loop, which we explain in the next section.

Homosexuals Are Cultural Beings

One of the puzzles surrounding Foucault's historical nominalism is why individuals would adopt an identity that was created to keep them down. Why would one want to identify with a depreciated category? One possible reason to adopt a reviled identity, Foucault believes, is that individuals can exploit this adoption, for example to claim their rights. This might be the case for Hacking's refugee women, too. Another answer is as straightforward but less satisfying: people adopt the homosexual identity because they are cultural beings, which means their identities are made up of the materials provided by their culture. These reasons may hold to some extent, but a mystery still remains: why is it that not every cultural identity is as easily adopted as an homosexuality? ...

[A]dopting the homosexual identity is not a "queer" choice, so to speak, even if it may now, under the present circumstances, marginalize someone. Same-sex sexual behavior is a behavior designed by natural selection to overcome marginalization and ostracism. Not every fringe person displays such behavior: some do, others do not. The point is, however, that if those who do display same-sex sexual behavior are further marginalized (due to their adoption of a depreciated identity), one can expect this behavior to become ever more frequent and intense. That is how a feedback loop is generated. The fact that homosexuals are marginalized because they have same-sex sexual contacts is, at least from an evolutionary point of view, quite ironic.

Animal biology suggest that same-sex sexual behavior between males has a long evolutionary history. Recent findings in history and anthropology suggest that such behavior was common in many human cultures all over the world. Many of the men who engaged in same-sex sexual practices were married and had children. It is only at the beginning of the 18th century that these men come to feel obliged to commit themselves either to same-sex sexuality *or* heterosexuality—a choice that is then thought to be determinant of their identity. Be that as it may, these recent trends have not diminished the occurence of occasional same-sex sexual behavior, as is evident from research in sexology ever since [Alfred] Kinsey['s research on sexuality in the 1940s]. Therefore, one could say that homosexuality is not a Darwinian paradox at all—it is "just" a social construction with a long evolutionary history.

Homosexuality Has Evolutionary Benefits to Individuals and Society

Joan Roughgarden

Joan Roughgarden is a professor of biology at Stanford University in California.

In June 1971 I marched in my first gay pride parade. I walked up Market Street in San Francisco, from the Civic Center to the Ferry Building. The parade was one of the biggest I had ever seen, and the sidewalks on both sides were packed six deep. I had heard that 1 in 10 people is gay or lesbian, but had always felt this number exaggerated. At this parade, though, I began to realise for the first time that the number of gays may indeed plausibly reach that figure.

This number of gay and lesbian people posed a problem to me as a biologist. My discipline teaches that homosexuality is some sort of unexplained anomaly. If the purpose of sexual contact is reproduction, as the standard explanation has it, how can all these gay people exist? One might argue they are somehow defective, that some developmental error or environmental influence has misdirected their sexual fantasies. If so, gay and lesbian people are here for a brief time during our species' evolution, awaiting removal when natural selection prunes those with lower Darwinian fitness.

Hmm. I began to wonder about the evolutionary puzzle of homosexuality. If a theory says something is wrong with so many people, then perhaps the theory is wrong, not the people.

Joan Roughgarden, "The In-crowd: Same-sex Relationships Are Not a Biological Dead End," *New Scientist*, issue 2430, January 17, 2004, pp. 36–39. Copyright © 2004 Reed Elsevier Business Publishing, Ltd. Reproduced by permission.

Sexual Selection Theory Is Wrong

But I feared I would have to leave the puzzle unsolved. In a few months I was to come out as a transgendered woman. I didn't know whether I would be fired from my professorship at Stanford University, California, and find myself working as a waitress in a transgender bar. In the event, I wasn't fired—although I was removed from all administrative responsibilities—and I wound up with more time to investigate how evolution has led to diverse manifestations of gender and sexuality.

Many animals, indeed, do not even sort neatly into two sexes at all.

I found that evolutionary theory had followed a wrong path that leads inexorably back to [Charles] Darwin—specifically to his theory of sexual selection, which I have concluded should be declared not only false but unfixable. Although I believe many biologists acknowledge that recent findings about gender and sexuality are problematic, few go as far as me in recommending that Darwin's theory of sexual selection be tossed out completely. So let me sketch the steps that have led me to this rather drastic and provocative conclusion—and to a better understanding of the biology of homosexuality and gender.

There are two glaring flaws in Darwin's thinking. In 1871 he wrote, "Females choose mates who are 'more attractive . . . vigorous and well-armed'" just as "man can give beauty . . . to his male poultry" by selective breeding. Hence the peacock's tail, Darwin's frequent example, is supposed to reflect peahen taste in male fashion, and antlers a preference for strong warrior stags. "Males of almost all animals have stronger passions than females," he wrote, and, "The female . . . with the rarest of exceptions is less eager than the male . . . she is coy." In

Darwin's view, males and females almost universally conform to their preordained roles of horny handsome warriors and discreetly discerning damsels.

But the real world is far more diverse than that. In many species, including ours, females are not necessarily less eager than males, nor do females all yearn for Arnold Schwarzenegger. Females often solicit males, and males often decline. Moreover, in many species the supposed sex roles reverse. Even Darwin acknowledged species of birds, like the jacana, in which the females are highly ornamented and the males dull and drab, reversing the peafowl story.

Some Animals Change Sex

Many animals, indeed, do not even sort neatly into two sexes at all. If you go snorkelling on a coral reef about one-third of the fish you see make both eggs and sperm at either the same time or different times during their lives. These are called simultaneous or sequential hermaphrodites respectively, and are said to "change sex" when they switch from making eggs to making sperm or vice versa. In fact the most common body plan among multicellular organisms, including plants, is for a single individual to make both male and female gametes at some time during their life. So the condition whereby an individual can be unambiguously classified as either male or female should not be considered the norm.

Social selection theory . . . provides a better explanation for much of the diversity we see in sexual practices.

Species may also feature more than one type of male and female. The multiple morphs of males in such species all produce sperm, but otherwise differ in body size, colour, morphology, behaviour and life history so much that an inexperienced naturalist might be tempted to classify them as different species. The same is true for multiple kinds of females that have nothing in common except that they all make eggs, such as yellow-throated and orange-throated side-blotched lizards, which lay eggs of different sizes.

I have termed these distinct morphs as "genders", and this terminology allows one to say there are more genders than sexes. The bluegill sunfish of the north-eastern US and Canada, for example, has three male genders that I term controllers, cooperators, and endrunners. The large, orange-breasted controllers and medium-sized cooperators, whose dark, barred colour pattern resembles that of females, court females jointly. The controller fertilises most of the eggs, but allows the cooperator a limited role as well. The small, pale endrunner males lurk in the weeds waiting to dash in while a female is laying her eggs and deposit some sperm of their own.

Sexual Contact Is Not About Reproduction

The second problem with Darwin's notion of sexual selection is that in relatively social species, such as most birds and mammals, sexual contact—mating—is not necessarily, indeed not even often, about the transfer of sperm. Mating is mostly directed at forming and managing relationships that may ultimately result in the successful production and rearing of offspring. A simple count of how many times mating takes place relative to the number of young born illustrates the point. In humans, for example, suppose Ozzie and Harriet have two children, have been married for 50 years, and make love regularly each week—say, Thursday night. After 50 years they will have mated over 2500 times, and produced two children, thus mating 1250 times per offspring produced. Sounds inefficient? Not if we suppose that regular mating allows the couple to stay together to successfully rear their two children. Similarly, in birds, primates, indeed everywhere, lots of mating occurs at times and places that cannot possibly result in immediate offspring production.

By this stage of my research I was beginning to suspect that Darwin might be all wrong about sex. It seemed to me that social organisation in animals revolves around the control of access to reproductive opportunity, which includes all the things that animals need to reproduce: food and nest sites, for instance, as well as mates. Animals make direct use of the resources they control, but may also use them as bargaining chips to buy the help of others. Furthermore, the dynamics of animal societies also involve decisions about where to allocate friendship and cooperation among animals of both the same sex and the other sex. Different arrangements of cooperative effort lead to the emergence of different structures for families and small groups.

Social Selection Theory

This theory, which I call social selection theory, provides a better explanation for much of the diversity we see in sexual practices. In bluegill sunfish, for example, social life does not, as traditional sexual selection theory requires, consist of females looking for males with great genes, or of males trying to fool females into thinking their genes are better than their neighbours'. Instead, it is about the ebb and flow of power to control access to reproductive opportunity. I suggest that controller males pay cooperator males for "marriage broker" services by allowing the cooperator to fertilise some of the eggs in his territory. In return, the cooperator male assists in courting females. Controller males without a cooperator male do not fare as well at attracting females. The feminine coloration pattern of the cooperator male may somehow promote this function, perhaps by allowing the cooperator male to develop a relationship with the females while the controller male is setting up and defending his territory.

The aspects of the relationships between animals that are managed by mating depend on the species' social system. Anthropologist Sarah Hrdy of the University of California at

Davis has shown that female monkeys in India mate with multiple males so that each will refrain from harming the young because he might be the father. In addition to managing male power, mating helps the pair bond and ensures that males deliver on their promise of parental investment, preventing them from becoming dead-beat dads.

Social selection theory also explains a puzzle that goes back all the way to Aristotle: the "penises" of female spotted hyenas. The female's clitoris is enlarged to the size of a male penis, and fat deposits in a nearby skin pouch resemble a scrotal sac. Females erect their penis many times during the day in interactions with other females. Sexual selection theory has no explanation for such an unusual characteristic that is not used in mate choice. I suggest, though, that a female spotted hyena that did not have a penis would be excluded from the female groups that control access to reproduction. This is an instance of what I call a social inclusionary trait: a trait that gains an individual admission to a social group, whether or not it has any other use. The human brain, with all its powerful capacity for conversation, art and music, may be another such trait.

Same-Sex Sexuality

Same-sex sexuality in female bonobos is another social inclusionary trait. I conjecture that females that do not participate regularly in mutual face-to-face genital rubbing do not form the bonds needed to participate in the groups that control access to food, or enjoy the protection necessary to raise young successfully.

Being upfront about how problematic sexual selection theory is may help curtail this misuse of biology.

Taken to its logical conclusion, this argument might imply that even classic sexual ornaments such as the peacock's tail or a stag's antlers are not there to attract females by advertising the bearer's virility. Instead, these traits may be intended for members of the same sex more than for the opposite sex. They may be badges of admission to membership in power-holding cliques. I am not aware of any experiments to test whether secondary sexual characters are really badges or ornaments. Some experiments have shown how modifying traits such as feather colours affects mate choice. I feel such experiments should also investigate how these modifications affect same-sex relationships, including membership in power-holding cliques.

This new perspective on animal social behaviour, and its rejection of Darwin's theory of sexual selection, undercuts the subject of evolutionary psychology. Many biologists are becoming increasingly uneasy at how psychologists have retooled sexual selection theory into a theory of human personality, complete with evolutionary rationales for everything from beauty to rape. Being upfront about how problematic sexual selection theory is may help curtail this misuse of biology.

Homosexuality Is Not an Aberrant Condition

I have now come full circle to the question I started with, the puzzle of homosexuality and gender, and the difficulty it poses for Darwinian sexual selection theory. Author Bruce Bagemihl, in his book *Biological Exuberance: Animal Homosexuality and Natural Diversity*, has catalogued over 300 vertebrate species in which same-sex genital contact regularly occurs. In some species, homosexuality is not very common—around 1 to 10 per cent of all mating. In others, such as bonobos, homosexual mating occurs as often as heterosexual mating. In some species only males participate, in others only females, in still others both sexes. Sometimes homosexuality is associated with pair bonds that last for years, and in others with short-term consortships. This broad occurrence of homosexuality among vertebrates raises the possibility that if it has a genetic basis at all, it has some broad adaptive significance, and is not an aberrant condition just a few species happen to be stuck with.

In humans, moreover, homosexuality is much too common for it to be considered a genetic aberration. Real genetic diseases are really rare, and their frequency inevitably depends on their severity. A disease that is uniformly lethal must arise anew each generation, so its frequency is equal to the mutation rate, say one in 1 million. A disease that causes only a 10 per cent drop in offspring production (fitness) is 10 times more common than a lethal disease—about one in 100,000. Similarly, a mere 1 per cent drop in fitness leads to a frequency of one in 10,000. If homosexuality has a frequency of 1 in 10, the fitness loss could be no more than 0.001 per cent, which is completely undetectable. A "common genetic disease" is a contradiction in terms, and homosexuality is three to four orders of magnitude more common than true genetic diseases such as Huntington's disease.

Homosexuality is a social inclusionary trait—that is, it provides animals, including perhaps humans at times, with admission to social groups.

Indeed, I challenge the presumption that homosexuality leads to any reduction in fitness whatever. Throughout history and across cultures, homoerotic attraction has not precluded heteroerotic attraction. And there is little evidence that people who feel homoerotic attraction have, as a group, any less Darwinian fitness than those who don't. After all, many exclusively heterosexual people do not have offspring either. Even if those with homoerotic attraction did have marginally fewer children, they might make up for it by a better chance of survival—during wars, for example, when homoerotic bonds might lead soldiers to protect one another more vigorously.

So what then, is the adaptive significance of homosexuality? Homosexuality has many uses, much as the ability to speak does. Homosexual contact is a way to communicate pleasure. And I suggest that homosexuality is a social inclusionary trait—that is, it provides animals, including perhaps humans at times, with admission to social groups. It evolves, I suggest, whenever same-sex cooperation helps achieve an evolutionarily successful life: to survive, find mates and protect one's young from harm. This plays out in different ways in different sexes and species. Sometimes, as with bonobos, same-sex cooperation provides group security and access to food that females need to successfully rear their young. For others, such as male Savanna baboons and probably some whales, it provides the allies they need to survive conflicts so that they may later mate. But the unifying principle is the same—homosexuality cements relationships that are crucial for a successful life.

Gay Sexual Identity Can Change with Religious Conversion

Tanya Erzen

Tanya Erzen is an assistant professor of comparative studies at Ohio State University in Columbus, Ohio.

In a run-down community center in San Rafael, California, a middle-aged man spoke haltingly in front of fifty people sitting on rickety folding chairs. As he testified to the power of Jesus in changing his life, there were murmurs of assent. He told the assembly, "I will never be the same again. I have closed the door." What would be a fairly normal evangelical church experience was transformed as he recounted his pornography addiction and his anonymous sexual encounters with other men. Rather than expressing shock or outrage, the members of the audience raised their arms and called out, "Praise him" and "Praise the Lord." Hank was one of a dozen men who had come to New Hope Ministry to rid themselves of homosexuality. At this annual Friends and Family conference, his testimony provided assurance to the gathering that after three years, he was a living example of the possibility for change.

Hopes of Healing Homosexuality

Listening raptly in the audience was a new member of the program. Curtis, twenty-one years old, with streaks of blond in his hair and numerous facial piercings, had arrived from Canada a month before. Raised in a nondenominational conservative Christian family of missionaries, Curtis believed that having same-sex desire was antithetical to living a Christian life. At age sixteen, he had come out to his family as "someone with gay feelings who wants to change." Instead of attending college, he had been involved in Christian youth groups since he was eighteen. Aside from a clandestine sexual relationship in high school, he had never allowed himself to date men. Eventually, with the encouragement of his parents and youth pastor, he decided that in order to conquer his same-sex attractions, he needed to devote himself to an ex-gay program. His ultimate goal was to overcome what he called his "homosexual problem" and eventually get married. "I don't want to be fifty years old, sitting in a gay bar because I just got dumped and have no kids, no family—and be lonelier than heck," he reasoned. Unable to secure a green card, Curtis was working in the New Hope ex-gay ministry administrative offices for the year. Whether filing or copying, he moved around the office tethered to a five-foot Walkman cable, listening to Christian techno music and reminiscing about his nights in the clubs of his hometown.

During the course of his year in the program, Curtis would experience moments of elation, severe depression, crushes on other men, homesickness, and boredom. He eventually would return home with the expectation that he would apply everything he had learned at New Hope to his old life in Canada. Instead, during the next several years he experienced only more uncertainty regarding his sexual struggles. He began occasionally dating men at the same time that he volunteered at a local ex-gay ministry. Later, he embarked upon a chaste relationship with a woman he hoped to marry, but he broke it off when he realized he could never be attracted to her sexually. Finally, he resumed his career as a hairdresser and moved from his rural hometown to Montreal, the first city he had ever lived in.

Curtis's story represents a familiar pattern for many ex-gay men and women who come to New Hope with the objective of healing their homosexuality, controlling sexual compulsions, becoming heterosexual, or even marrying someone of the opposite sex. Curtis arrived with the idea that, after a year, his homosexual struggle would subside. He left feeling stronger in his Christian identity, but not necessarily with diminished homosexual urges. It was through religious growth that he believed he would eventually conquer his attractions to men. Struggling with these attractions his entire life was acceptable to him. He reasoned that his faith in God would sustain him and provide him with hope that change was possible.

All those in attendance believed that through Christian faith, religious conversion, and a daily accountable relationship with one another and with God they could heal their homosexuality.

Sexual and Spiritual Conversion

The controversy around the ex-gay movement has tended to fixate on whether people can change their sexuality. In their testimonies, Hank and Curtis both swore they were altered people, but their assertions encompass a range of possibilities for change that do not necessarily include sexual orientation, behaviors, or desires. When they spoke of personal transformation, they were more likely to refer to their religious identities and sense of masculinity. Christian Right groups claim that men and women can become heterosexuals, and they present men like Hank as confirmation. Opponents of the ex-gay movement argue, based on their evidence of the men and women who have left ex-gay ministries to live as gay- or lesbian-identified, that ex-gay men and women are simply controlling their behavior and repressing their desires. Both sides neglect the centrality of the religious belief system and personal experiences that impel men and women to spend years in ex-gay ministries. Rather than definitive change, ex-gays undergo a conversion process that has no endpoint, and they acknowledge that change encompasses desires, behavior, and identities that do not always align neatly or remain fixed. Even the label "ex-gay" represents their sense of being in flux between identities.

While many conservative Christian churches and organizations condemn homosexuality, New Hope Ministry represents a unique form of nondenominational Christian practice focused specifically on sexuality. New Hope combines psychological, therapeutic, and biblical approaches in an effort to change and convert gay men and lesbians to nonhomosexual Christian lives. Unlike previous Christian movements in the United States, the ex-gay movement, of which New Hope Ministry is a part, explicitly connects sexual and religious conversion, placing sexuality at the core of religious identity. By becoming a born-again Christian and maintaining a personal relationship with Jesus, ex-gay men and women are born again religiously, and as part of that process they consider themselves reconstituted sexually. They grapple with a seemingly irreconcilable conflict between their conservative Christian beliefs and their own same-sex desires. In their worldview, an ex-gay ministry becomes a place where these dual identities are rendered temporarily compatible. Their literal belief that the Bible condemns homosexual practices and identity leads them to measure their success in negotiating their new identities through submission and surrender to Jesus in all things. Even if desires and attractions remain after they have attended an ex-gay ministry like New Hope, their relationship with God and Jesus continues intact. That relationship supersedes any sexual changes, minimizing their frustration and disillusionment when the longed for sexual changes do not occur. In the words of Curtis, "Heterosexuality isn't the goal; giving our hearts and being obedient to God is the goal."

New Hope Ministry

New Hope Ministry is the oldest of five residential ex-gay programs in the United States. Frank Worthen formed New Hope in 1973 after a revelation in which God exhorted him to abandon homosexuality. With the help of a board of directors and house leaders who have successfully completed the program, Frank, a spry man in his mid-seventies who still jets around in a cherry-red convertible, oversees New Hope, teaches classes to the men in the program, and serves as an assistant pastor in an ex-gay-affiliated church called Church of the Open Door. His wife of over twenty years, Anita, spearheads a ministry for parents of gay children from the same office. She is not an ex-gay but the mother of a gay son. Frank and Anita live a few minutes away from the residential program in a tiny but immaculate studio apartment. After two decades of marriage, they are paragons for other Christian men and women who pray that they will also get married. New Hope is now one of hundreds of evangelical Christian ministries in the United States and abroad where men and women attend therapy sessions, Bible studies, twelve-step-style meetings, and regular church services as part of their "journey out of homosexuality." . . .

Although there were a few men from mainline Protestant denominations and one Catholic in the program, at some point most had become involved in an evangelical form of Christianity and undergone a born-again experience. All of the New Hope participants maintained a personal relationship with Jesus and believed to differing degrees in the infallibility and literal truth of biblical scripture. With few exceptions, the informal, experiential religious style of New Hope and Church of the Open Door was familiar to them. All those in attendance believed that through Christian faith, religious conversion, and a daily accountable relationship with one another and with God they could heal their homosexuality. Desires or attractions might linger for years, but they would emerge with new religious identities and the promise that faith and their relationships with one another and God would eventually transform them. . . .

Broken Individuals

New Hope accepts what the ex-gay movement calls "broken" individuals as long as they are invested in the process of religious and sexual conversion. I argue that by combining biblical, developmental, and twelve-step principles, New Hope also creates new familial and kinship arrangements and networks of ex-gays. The ministry's close-knit, highly regulated programs foster a sense of religious belonging based on same-sex bonds rather than the conservative Christian ideal of heterosexual marriage. The ministries also function as unlikely havens for those banned from conservative churches and alienated from family members and even from gay organizations or social networks. Individuals remain affiliated with ex-gay ministries for years because they offer religious belonging, acceptance, and accountability. Ex-gay ministries flourish because the men and women grappling with same-sex behavior and attraction desperately want to locate themselves in a supportive cultural world. Places like New Hope provide the material conditions for community in addition to a more diffuse sense of religious and sexual belonging and kinship. In conversations, the men and women at New Hope invoked a utopian aspect to their chosen families: some men even referred to finding a sense of belonging at New Hope as a coming-out process. In many ways, the community and religious aspects of the program became more important than any sexual changes they experienced.

Many ex-gays admit that although some changes in behavior and identity take place, it is more probable that they will continue as "strugglers" their entire lives.

While individuals at New Hope understand the transformation of their sexual identities as a choice and a right, organizations of the Christian Right have utilized their testimonies as living proof that homosexuality is merely a choice, a developmental disorder, or a lifestyle, promoting a wider anti-gay agenda cloaked in the rhetoric of choice, change, and compassion. Organizations of the Christian Right exploit the example of ex-gay conversion to counter legislative proposals that would grant workplace protection, partner benefits, adoption rights, and health care to gay men and lesbians. Rather than explicit anti-gay rhetoric, groups like Focus on the Family and the American Family Association frame the debate over change in terms of "hope for healing," despite that fact that ex-gays' testimonies and queer conversions often contradict these politics. The ex-gay movement has internal fissures and disagreements, even as the national leadership attempts to maintain the pretense of unity. Concentrating on individual testimonies illuminated the disparities between ground-level participants, ministry leaders, and Christian Right organizations. It also exposed why some men and women become disillusioned with ministries. This cynicism was borne out in the ways ex-gay men and women I talked to disassociated themselves from the politics of the Christian Right and even the leadership of the ex-gay movement. Some men and women in ex-gay ministries resent that the wider ex-gay movement showcases and distorts their stories to promote an anti-gay political agenda. Many ex-gays admit that although some changes in behavior and identity take place, it is more probable that they will continue as "strugglers" their entire lives.

People Do Not Choose Their Sexual Orientation

John Corvino

John Corvino, who teaches philosophy at Wayne State University in Detroit, Michigan, writes biweekly for Between the Lines.

One of the most persistent debates surrounding homosexuality regards whether gays are "born that way" or whether homosexuality is a "chosen lifestyle."

The debate is ill-formed from the start, in that it conflates two separate questions:

1. How did you become what you are? (By genetics? Early environment? Willful choice? Some combination of the above?), and

2. Can you change what you are?

Sexual Orientation Is Not a Choice

The answers to these two questions vary independently. My dark hair color is genetically determined, but I can change it (though I'd make a rather frightful blonde). The fact that my native language is English is environmentally determined, but I can't change it. (I can learn a new language, of course, but at this stage it would never have the character of my native language.)

The fact that I put the last sentence in parentheses is a matter of willful choice, and, like most matters of willful choice, it can be changed (although my editors had better leave it alone if they know what's good for them). Still, some choices are not so easily undone.

John Corvino, "Nature? Nurture? It Doesn't Matter," *Between the Lines*, August 12, 2004. Reproduced by permission.

Having chosen never to practice piano as a child, it would be possible, but rather challenging, for me to become proficient at piano now.

I never chose to "become gay," and I'm not even sure how one would go about doing so.

Of course, sexual orientation is not like piano-playing. I never turned down "straight lessons" as a child. ("No, Mommy, I wanna play with my Easy-Bake oven instead!") I never chose to "become gay," and I'm not even sure how one would go about doing so. We do not choose our romantic feelings— indeed, we often find them thrust upon us at surprising and inopportune times. We discover them; we do not invent them.

We Are Not Born This Way

So we must be born this way, right? Wrong. For several reasons. No one is born with romantic feelings, much less engaging in sexual conduct. That comes later. Whether it comes as a result of genetics, or early environment, or watching too many episodes of Wonder Woman is a separate question that can't be settled by simple introspection.

Moreover, the fact that feelings are strong doesn't mean that they're genetically determined. They might be, but they might not. Sexual orientation's involuntariness, which is largely beyond dispute, is separate from its origin, which is still controversial, even among sympathetic scientists.

But here's the good news: *It doesn't matter* whether we're born this way. A lot of gay-rights advocates seem to think otherwise. They worry that if we're not "born this way," then homosexuality would be "unnatural" in some morally significant sense.

Nonsense. Again: the fact that I speak English rather than French is learned behavior, but it does not follow that my doing so is unnatural or in need of reparative therapy.

Did God Make Us This Way?

But wouldn't a genetic basis for homosexuality prove that God made us this way? No, it wouldn't—at least not in any helpful sense. Put aside the difficulties about establishing God's existence or discerning divine intentions. The fact is that there are plenty of genetically influenced traits that are nevertheless undesirable. Alcoholism may have a genetic basis, but it doesn't follow that alcoholics ought to drink excessively. Some people may have a genetic predisposition to violence, but they have no more right to attack their neighbors than anyone else. Persons with such tendencies cannot say "God made me this way" as an excuse for acting on their dispositions.

This is not to say that we shouldn't frequently remind people that homosexuality ... is a deep, important, and relatively fixed feature of human personality.

"Whoa!" you might object. "Are you saying that homosexuality is a disorder like alcoholism?" Not at all. The difference between alcoholism and homosexuality is that alcoholism has inherently bad effects whereas homosexuality does not. But this distinction just reinforces my point: we do not determine whether a trait is good by looking at where it came from (genetics, environment, or something else). We determine whether it is good by looking at its effects.

Why We Are Homosexual Is Irrelevant

Nor does it matter whether sexual orientation can be changed. For even if it could (which is doubtful in most cases), it doesn't follow that it should. Much like my hair color.

Remember: bad arguments in favor of a good cause are still bad arguments—and in the long run not very good for the cause. This is not to say that we shouldn't frequently remind people that homosexuality, like heterosexuality, is a deep, important, and relatively fixed feature of human personality. It's just that those facts can only get us so far. In a 1964 speech to the New York Mattachine Society, an early gay rights group, activist Frank Kameny announced:

> We are interested in obtaining rights for our respective minorities as Negroes, as Jews, and as Homosexuals. Why we are Negroes, Jews, or Homosexuals is totally irrelevant, and whether we can be changed to Whites, Christians or heterosexuals is equally irrelevant.

Kameny (who is still going strong at 79) was absolutely right. Too bad people still haven't gotten the message.

CHAPTER 2

Do People with Alternative Lifestyles Face Serious Discrimination?

Chapter Preface

In 1996, the United States Supreme Court, in *Romer v. Evans* (517 U.S. 620), ruled for the first time that gay and lesbian people are protected by the equal protection clause of the federal constitution. This decision is perhaps the most significant legal victory to date for the gay and lesbian movement. The central issue in the case was whether or not local communities (i.e. Aspen, Boulder, and Denver) could enact antidiscrimination ordinances that included gays and lesbians. These local ordinances prohibited discrimination in housing, employment, education, public accommodations, health and welfare services, and other activities based specifically on sexual orientation.

The passage of these ordinances greatly alarmed an influential socially conservative grassroots group called Colorado for Family Values. The religious organization worried that the local ordinances both legitimized homosexual conduct and threatened traditional family values. Unable to locally overturn the ordinances, the group sought to reverse them through the statewide referendum process. By collecting enough petition signatures, Colorado for Family Values placed the issue before the electorate in the form of a constitutional amendment. The amendment, which was called Amendment 2, would have repealed all sections in existing city and statewide laws and policies that specifically protected gay people from discrimination, and prevented all branches of Colorado state and local government from enacting or enforcing any such measures in the future.

In 1993, a majority of state voters agreed with Colorado for Family Values by passing the state constitutional amendment to exclude gays and lesbians from all antidiscrimination laws and policies. The ballot measure passed 53 percent to 47 percent. To the surprise of no one, the case was appealed to the Colorado Supreme Court. Later that year, the high court ruled that the amendment violated the equal protection clause of the 14th Amendment to the United States insofar as it denied gays equal rights to normal political processes. Afterward, Colorado Attorney General Gale Norton appealed the ruling to the United States Supreme Court. Her argument was fourfold: (1) Amendment 2 did not treat gays and lesbians differently. It only eliminated laws and policies that granted them special rights; (2) gays and lesbians, unlike racial minorities, did not need special rights because they were better educated, wealthier, and more politically organized than other segments of the population; (3) the amendment did not deprive gays and lesbians of political rights for they could continue to form political organizations, run for office, and cast ballots; (4) the high court was bound to respect the peoples' judgment, especially since the measure followed the common practice of giving state governments broad authority over cities and municipalities.

In *Romer v. Evans*, (the former being Roy Romer, the governor at the time, and the latter being Richard Evans, a gay activist and the coordinator of Denver's HIV resource program), opponents of the measure argued that the state amendment violated the equal protection clause of the United States Constitution's 14th Amendment, which says: "No state shall . . . deny to any person within its jurisdiction the equal protection of the laws." The amendment singled out gays and lesbians and intentionally denied them of their right to utilize regular political institutions like city councils to enact laws and policies protecting themselves from discrimination. Moreover, these critics claimed that homosexuals had experienced widespread hostility and discrimination. They maintained that national studies showed that homosexuals were the victims of more hate crimes than any other minority.

In May 1996 the United States Supreme Court, in a 6-3 decision, ruled Colorado's Amendment 2 unconstitutional.

Justice Anthony Kennedy, who wrote the majority opinion, rejected the state's "special rights" argument. He opined that antidiscrimination protection was not a "special right" because such laws protected fundamental rights already enjoyed by all other citizens. He also implied that the amendment's passage was born of a "bare . . . desire to harm homosexuals." In dissent, Justice Antonin Scalia wrote that Amendment 2 was "a modest attempt by seemingly tolerant Coloradans to preserve traditional sexual mores against the efforts of a politically powerful minority to revise those mores through use of the laws." The amendment did not deny homosexuals access to the political process, but "merely made it more difficult to enact laws that they favored." Moreover, Scalia accused the court of judicial activism. "Since the constitution of the United States says nothing about this subject, it is left to be resolved by normal democratic means, including the democratic adoption of provisions in state constitutions."

Following the *Romer* ruling, a large number of local governments across the nation expanded the legal rights of gays and lesbians. By 2005, eleven states, twenty-seven counties, and more than 150 municipalities had passed laws protecting gays and lesbians from discrimination. Most of these laws were limited to prohibiting workplace discrimination. A few laws, however, were more expansive, preventing gay discrimination by public accommodations, credit institutions, healthcare providers, educational facilities, and landlords.

Homosexuals Treat Bisexuals with Disdain

Joy Morgenstern

Joy Morgenstern is a freelance writer.

Many of us can remember a time when misconceptions about gay people were practically universal. In those days, most straight people assumed gays to be mentally ill, and most likely child molesters. Some straight people who didn't think gay people were crazy or evil still believed the stereotypes: gay men were all limp-wristed girly men and lesbians were all big, tough wannabe men.

A lot of the world still, unfortunately, thinks of gay people in these terms, but I think most of us would agree that things have improved quite a bit since the advent of the gay rights movement.

Gays Discriminate Against Bisexuals

Bisexuals encounter the same sorts of prejudice as gay people. However, we encounter it within the gay community as well as in the straight world. Most bisexuals I've spoken to experience feeling misunderstood and ostracized by both gay and straight people. A lot of us feel angry that many members of the gay community are unwilling to understand or accept us, and sometimes treat us with the same disdain with which the straight world has treated gays.

We feel even more hurt when gays reject us than when straights do, since we feel that gay people should know better. Many bisexuals have fought on the front lines of the gay rights movement, yet it seems like we have only token representation in the community; the word "bisexual" has been added to the masthead, but we don't feel truly included or accepted.

Being Invisible

Sometimes the problem is just that we're invisible: when we're involved with someone of the opposite sex everyone assumes we're straight, and when we're involved with someone of the same sex, everyone assumes we're gay. Many people, both gay and straight, are perfectly accepting of our bisexuality once we explain it to them. But the feelings of being misunderstood and rejected seem to be so common, at least among the bisexual women I've talked to, that I think we need to take a look at some of the myths we encounter over and over again.

Bisexuals Are Not Promiscuous

A lot of people seem to think that saying "I'm bisexual" is another way of saying "I'll sleep with anyone." There are, undoubtedly, bisexual people who will sleep with anyone, just as there are straight and gay people who will sleep with anyone. But this type of terminal horniness is no more common among bisexuals than in any other group. Just because a woman identifies as bi does not mean she's a promiscuous, unfaithful slut who will leave you for a man. Besides, what lesbian hasn't met promiscuous, unfaithful lesbians who dump their girlfriends for other women? (Of course you have, although I hope for your sake not too often.)

Women who do not identify as lesbians . . . are branded as traitors, turncoats, and betrayers of the greater sisterhood.

There are lots and lots of bisexual people. Some are indeed sleazy and over-sexed. However, most of us are ordinary people whose sexual attraction to both men and women is a significant enough part of our lives that we just don't feel right calling ourselves either straight or gay. And just because we're potentially attracted to, well, everyone, doesn't mean that we are any more sexually active than anyone else. Some of us are promiscuous. Some of us are involved in long-term, monogamous relationships. Some of us have not had a date in years (sigh). Some of us are hardly ever attracted to anyone, so when that rare event happens, gender just isn't important. Most of us, like most gay and straight people, want to be with That Certain Someone. The only difference between us and everyone else is that we're open to finding either Mr. or Ms. Right.

Bisexuals Are Not Gender Liars

Most people define themselves as either gay or straight. Since most people are predominantly attracted to people only of one sex, a lot of them just cannot believe that some of us are attracted to both. They think that we must be lying; we are people who just can't admit we're gay. They say things to us like: "Pick a lane." or "Choose a team." And, my personal favorite: "Just because you sleep with men sometimes doesn't give you the right to deny you're a lesbian."

While there are people who temporarily call themselves bisexual at some point during their journey to self-awareness, most bisexuals are not transitioning anywhere. Just because some of us seem to be more attracted to women than to men, or vice versa, does not mean that we are not bisexual. Being bisexual does not mean that someone is exactly, equally attracted to both men and women. Some of us are more attracted to one sex, while some of us are equally attracted to both. Some of us are attracted to both very macho men *and* very femme females, whereas some of us are attracted to androgyny. Some of us have never actually had a gay relationship, or a straight relationship. Some of us find that our relative attraction to either sex changes with time. Every bisexual woman I've talked to seems to have different desires, views and goals.

Bisexuals Are Not Gay Traitors

Some lesbians seem to feel that their sexuality is a political statement. Therefore, women who do not identify as lesbians, especially women who sometimes have relationships with other women, are branded as traitors, turncoats and betrayers of the greater sisterhood. I have been told that my relationships with men are simply "wrong," which sounds disturbingly like what [Rev.] Jerry Falwell says about all of us.

For most of us, bisexuality represents openness to loving both men and women, not a compulsion to do so every night.

I agree that being out, being open about who you are, and having pride, especially in the face of prejudice, are political statements. But I just don't believe that anyone's sexuality, in and of itself, is political. It's what you do with it and how you present it and deal with it that's political. I have met many women who are occasionally, or even frequently, attracted to men but still define themselves as lesbians because they feel that their relationships with women are the primary motivating force in their lives. And I recognize that this motivation can be political as well as emotional. However, that does not mean that all women who are attracted to women feel the same way. If you feel right defining yourself as a lesbian, even if you are attracted to men a tiny bit or a little bit or a lot, that's your decision. Just don't make that decision for me, too.

Bisexuals Are Like Everyone Else

It's true that some bisexuals are not satisfied unless they regularly have sex with both men and women. Is that really all that different or all that more unusual, than any type of person who feels the need to have multiple sex partners? For most of us, bisexuality represents openness to loving both men and women, not a compulsion to do so every night.

In the end, we're just like everyone else. We want to love who we love, be attracted to who we're attracted to, fall in love with someone who will make us happy. And just like most people, we don't want to feel like we're living a lie or stuck in the closet. we're here, and we're queer too, so get used to us. Think about it, won't you?

Radical Islam Is More of a Threat to Gays than Christian Fundamentalism

Christopher Lisotta

Christopher Lisotta is a freelance writer in Los Angeles.

Kristine Withers was feeling threatened by the Islamic Thinkers Society when she was arrested for getting into an altercation with the radical group in July 2004. The militants had become a weekly fixture on a street corner near her home in the Jackson Heights neighborhood of New York City's Queens, setting up tables and erecting signs with messages reading "Your terrorists are our heroes" and "Allah will destroy nations that allow homosexuality."

Radical Islam Is a Real Threat

Since then the 43-year-old lesbian has had several run-ins with the group and has been admonished by authorities to be more tolerant. Indeed, Withers has been somewhat hostile. But that's what's needed, she argues, given the incredible threat the Islamic Thinkers pose to the well-being of the neighborhood's sizable gay and lesbian population. "They think they own the neighborhood, and the cops give them the attitude that they do," she says. "I'm very concerned."

After another altercation in January—during which Withers claims she was knocked to the ground—Withers was charged with disorderly conduct. In April the charges were dismissed. "For some reason the 115th precinct and local politicians turn their backs," she says. "They are afraid. And gay organizations? No response. It's all out of fear."

Withers's confrontations with the Islamic Thinkers may seem relatively minor, but they have brought major media at-

Christopher Lisotta, "Radical Islam in Your Backyard," *The Advocate*, May 23, 2006, pp. 30–32. www.advocate.com. Reproduced by permission.

tention to the presence of radical Islam in the United States and its impassioned and sometimes violent opposition to freedom of the press, women's rights, and homosexuality. When worldwide protests erupted over the publication of cartoons in Denmark depicting the prophet Muhammad, the Islamic Thinkers, who have ties to the radical Muslim group Al-Muhajiroun, were among the more than 1,000 Muslims protesting in Manhattan near the Danish consulate on February 17. They carried signs portraying George W. Bush and Danish editor Flemming Rose (who had made the initial decision to run the cartoons in *Jyllands-Posten*) with targets on their foreheads.

European Islam Is More Radical

Groups like the Islamic Thinkers are not nearly as prevalent in the United States as they are in the European Union, where many Muslim residents subscribe to a much more radical interpretation of Islam. In the Netherlands in recent years Islam has been colliding with the country's open acceptance of homosexuality. There have been numerous reports of gay bashings and other violent crimes, including the 2005 gay-bashing of *Washington Blade* executive editor Chris Crain by a group of youths who were reportedly of Moroccan descent. And gays and lesbians in Amsterdam said in a recent survey they don't feel as safe as they once did and that overall tolerance of homosexuality is in decline.

But that hasn't happened in the United States—not yet, anyway. When it comes to the rights of LGBT [lesbian, gay, bisexual, transgendered] people in the United States, radical Islam is a far more dangerous threat than fundamentalist Christianity, claims Claire Berlinski, the author of *Menace in Europe: Why the Continent's Crisis Is America's Too*. "It's the most pressing threat to liberty right now. They really do think Western civilization would be best brought to an end. Anyone considered an apostate is very much at risk."

A Tough Stance Is Required

Berlinski understands that taking such a hard line could make her sound racist and intolerant, but the rhetoric coming from radical Islamists—some of whom espouse the full implementation of Islamic sharia law, reduced rights for women, and death for gays and lesbians—requires a strong stand. "It sounds so strange coming out of my mouth, but it's the only reasonable thing you can conclude when confronted with someone who wants you dead," she says.

Americans, especially gay Americans, can't afford to ignore what's going on.

Berlinski has been a vocal critic of those who seem to take a soft approach to radical Islamists. She points to the assassination attempt on openly gay Paris mayor Bertrand Delanoë, who was stabbed at an all-night celebration at the Paris city hall in October 2002. The press made little mention of the fact that the assassin, Azedine Berkane, was a Muslim of Algerian descent who had openly expressed his hatred of politicians and gays.

But Faisal Alam, cofounder of Al-Fatiha, a national LGBT support group for Muslims trying to reconcile their sexuality with their faith, cautions that gays and lesbians shouldn't see all Muslims as threats. "We should have more dialogue within our community and education for a religion that remains mystifying in some people's minds," he says.

The latest book by former *Advocate* reporter Bruce Bawer, *While Europe Slept: How Radical Islam Is Destroying the West From Within*, includes personal accounts of intimidation by radical Islamists in his adopted home of Norway and profiles how appeasement of religious extremism is a huge risk for the West.

Gay Americans Must Remain Alert

Bawer also cautions against lumping Muslims together. There isn't nearly as much radicalism in the United States because many of the country's estimated 5 million to 7 million Muslims are native converts, which don't compare to Western Europe's much larger, immigrant-dominated Muslim population. "Muslims emigrating to the United States tend to be more educated, less religious, and readier to integrate and to work than Muslims emigrating to Europe," he says. "Plus, Americans—believe it or not—are far better than Europeans at giving immigrants jobs and accepting them as equals."

> *Progress can be made by forming alliances with moderate Muslims who have differing opinions on the rights of women and gays.*

But Americans need to be more aware of what radical Islam espouses, he adds. "Americans, especially gay Americans, can't afford to ignore what's going on," Bawer says. "Christianity began to reform itself centuries ago. Islam has yet to begin the process. Many Christian churches are gay-friendly. *Gay-friendly mosque* is still an oxymoron."

And the ability of Muslims to integrate comes with a potential price for LGBT Americans, Bawer warns. "Because immigrants fit in so quickly in the United States, it takes less time than in Europe for an immigrant group to become a political force," he says, "and the idea of American Muslims becoming a political force along the lines of the Christian right is a prospect that we should all be focused on, and deeply concerned about."

Gays Should Ally with Moderate Muslims

Asra Nomani, the author of *Standing Alone in Mecca: An American Woman's Struggle for the Soul of Islam*, doesn't see

American Muslims becoming an antigay force because they have other issues to worry about in a post-September 11 world.

"American Muslims are basically too afraid to take their homophobia into action," Nomani says, agreeing with Bawer that some kind of Islamic reformation has yet to happen. "We haven't had the advances the Christians and Jews have had with new interpretations—we are just on the verge of that," she says, adding that you still "touch a nerve if you raise the idea that Islam does not condemn homosexuality."

That's true, says Alam, who is hoping to spur a discussion about homosexuality by reaching out to large Muslim organizations in the United States, such as the Council of American-Islamic Relations and the Islamic Society of North America. "All of them know we exist; some we've had conversations with," Alam says. "For the most part, what they say is, 'We don't agree with what you're doing, but we're not going to stop it.'"

Progress can be made by forming alliances with moderate Muslims who have differing opinions on the rights of women and gays and are starting to speak out, Alam says. "It's a terrifying time, but it's also an amazing time," he says. "Reform in Islam is emerging. Fundamentalists are also solidifying themselves, which is why you see such violent reactions. Muslims who have sat on the fence are starting to take sides."

Abdullah has spoken out against tolerating Muslims who come to the United States and subscribe to a reversal of the rights and liberties Americans—including gays— have come to expect.

Nomani too believes progress in combating radicalism is possible. She has been leading a movement in the United States to allow women to pray with men in the main hall of mosques, a movement that has brought a few death threats.

And she connects the rights of women within Islam with the rights of all sexual minorities. "I'm personally committed to arguing theologically the acceptance of gays and lesbians in the Muslim world," she says, "and scholars are out there doing it quietly. We are going to continue to chip away at it."

Gays Must Defend Freedom

Imam Daaylee Abdullah converted to Islam as an adult after being introduced to the religion in China, where the Muslims he met did not practice the fundamentalist Wahhabi form of the religion more common in the Middle East. While getting an Islamic law degree at the Graduate School of Islamic Social Sciences in Leesburg, Va., Abdullah's homosexuality became known to school administrators, who forced him out before he could finish. For the past seven years Abdullah has run the Yahoo group MuslimGayMen, which started with a few hundred members but has grown to more than 1,200. They discuss everything from how to come out to family and friends to learning more about Islamic law.

Since Christianity, Judaism, and Islam grew out of the same Abrahamic tradition, Abdullah argues, "that shows the inclusiveness of what God's concept is. God always talks in broad terms anyway, and the Koran teaches that."

Abdullah has spoken out against tolerating Muslims who come to the United States and subscribe to a reversal of the rights and liberties Americans—including gays—have come to expect. "They cannot make it Islam only," Abdullah says. "They want the economic benefits but not the social interactions."

The LGBT community has always been a cultural leader in terms of new thought for society, Abdullah says, and they shouldn't be afraid of offering a full-throated defense of fundamental freedoms. "We need to speak up," he says. "Let's not be drowned out by the screams and hollering."

Back in Jackson Heights, that's what Withers says she is doing when she encounters members of the Islamic Thinkers

Society, who like to stand on the sidewalk and shout condemnations of the West in Arabic. And she hopes other gays and lesbians will wake up to the potential problem. "The community needs to be thinking about [radical Islam] a lot more," she says. "It's definitely going to grow."

Homophobia Stems from Unquestioned Religious Faith

Peter S. Cahn

Peter S. Cahn is an assistant professor of anthropology at the University of Oklahoma in Norman.

Choosing career over lifestyle, I packed my Honda on the blue shores of the Pacific and pointed it to the red heart of America. Before then Oklahoma had entered my consciousness as a concrete place only twice: when I read *The Grapes of Wrath* in high school, and in the wake of the 1995 bombing in Oklahoma City. Neither produced many positive associations with the state I was about to call home. Neither signaled a welcoming place for gay man.

When I arrived in 2002, I heard news that confirmed my impression. A local gay-rights group had sued Oklahoma City after municipal officials rejected the group's request to display rainbow banners from city-owned light posts. Earlier the mayor had defended his position by saying that if the city could not hang banners with a religious message, then it should not be required to promote an "irreligious message." A federal judge disagreed, ruling the rejection an infringement of free speech and ordering the banners replaced in time for gay and lesbian history month.

Oklahoman Gays Are Harassed

Even with legal protection, gays and lesbians in Oklahoma have to contend with continuing harassment, I learned. Protestors set up pickets along a strip of gay nightclubs in Oklahoma City. Some teenagers who come out to their parents are sent to coercive Christian-sponsored therapy programs to cure

Peter S. Cahn, "A Gay Scholar Confronts the Harshness of the Heartland," *The Chronicle of Higher Education*, vol. 53, no. 6, September 29, 2006. Copyright © 2006 by *The Chronicle of Higher Education*. Reproduced by permission.

their homosexual urges. An openly gay candidate for county commissioner faced a ruthless campaign targeting his "values."

Ensconced at the university, I felt insulated from this assault. My colleagues always behaved professionally, and I developed a small network of other out faculty and staff members. Besides, I could camouflage myself easily. I was in my late 20s and unmarried, fairly common these days. My car bumper featured an array of stickers for Democratic candidates, but no rainbow symbols. Moreover, my research on evangelical Christianity in Mexico rarely touched on gay themes. Even though I never denied my sexuality and always included material on sexuality in general in my anthropology courses, being gay did not seem relevant to my academic role at the university.

Antigay Legislation

That changed in the run-up to the 2004 elections. That year the Oklahoma Legislature considered 10 antigay measures, including some that sought to restrict same-sex marriage. Never mind that Oklahoma as well as the federal government had already passed so-called defense-of-marriage acts. Bill Graves, then a Republican state representative from Oklahoma City, was a cosponsor of a successful bill proposing a state constitutional amendment limiting marriage to one man and one woman.

Mr. Graves has asserted that "in Western civilization and in all recorded civilizations of the world, marriage has always been viewed as a union between a man and a woman." By basing his opposition to same-sex marriage on anthropological evidence, the legislator presented an opportunity for me to defend gay rights on intellectual grounds. As any cultural-anthropology class will teach, marriage across time and space has more to do with status and alliances than romantic love between two individuals of the opposite sex. In fact, Mr. Graves had it exactly backward. Favoring the union between one man and one woman is a relatively recent and localized innovation in the history of marriage.

Before the fall elections, which included the proposed constitutional amendment against same-sex marriage, a graduate-student group organized a panel discussion to examine the issue. The group invited me to give the social-science perspective, a political philosopher to provide an ethical context, and Mr. Graves to defend his legislation. The organizers blitzed the campus media and booked a room in the student union that held 200 people.

Debating Gay Marriage

On the day of the event, the crowd overflowed the space. Before it began, I shook hands with Mr. Graves, a courtly, older gentleman sporting the American flag lapel pin that all politicians seem obligated to wear. As he pleasantly chatted about his memories of the university with me, I realized that he had no idea which side of the issue I was on or even that I was one of the sinful gays he ranted about on the floor of the state House of Representatives.

Fundamentalist religions favor obedience to doctrine over independent thought.

As it turned out, I spoke first, and Mr. Graves followed me. I had the advantage of knowing what he would argue, so I tried to pre-empt his logic by presenting examples of flexible marriage arrangements. I described the precedent for same-sex marriage in the anthropological record among some Native American groups. I closed by warning against the dangers of ethnocentrism—the tendency to hold the beliefs of your own culture as the norm. Anthropological evidence undermines, not upholds, the case for restricting marriage to a single form.

Mr. Graves spoke without notes and without acknowledging anything I had said. He began by repeating the assertion that marriage between a man and a woman constituted the bedrock of society's existence. Attempts to "redefine" marriage chip away at the core values underpinning this country, he said. To some hissing from the audience, he explained that Christian principles as reflected in the Holy Bible have guided lawmakers from the inception of the United States. Since the Bible makes clear that "homosexuality is an abomination in God's eyes," it is not bigotry to deny gays the right to marry; rather, he argued, it is defending the divine order.

During the question-and-answer period, I received the typical question about how allowing gays to marry could be a slippery slope to bestiality, but most of the audience targeted Mr. Graves. One young woman who identified herself as an Oklahoman and a Jew wondered how legislators could represent non-Christian citizens. That touched off a technical discussion between Mr. Graves and the philosopher about the founding fathers and the separation of church and state.

Legal Discrimination Against Gays

At the end of the event, Mr. Graves shook my hand again. I couldn't help feeling envious of his total self-confidence, his imperviousness to criticism.

He knew that as a grandfatherly, heterosexual, white Christian, he would never have to feel the sting of public denunciation for his "lifestyle." I, on the other hand, lived in a state where my elected representatives considered it acceptable to discriminate against me. I could take some consolation in the audience's negative reaction to the legislator, but I found it disheartening that no amount of reasoning could change his mind.

In my academic bubble, I would mark down Mr. Graves's presentation for failing to provide testable evidence to support his claims. The currency of scholarly exchange is argument and proof. By contrast, the political world operates on nebulous values and bold assertions. Since legislators like Mr. Graves do not gather and weigh evidence to arrive at their positions, exposure to contradictory examples has no effect on their thinking.

Fundamentalist Religions Spurn Independent Thought

While academics expect their arguments to change over time as new evidence comes to light, politicians worry about accusations of weakness if they modify their stances. This attitude mirrors the logic of faith. As I saw while conducting research with Mexican converts from Roman Catholicism to evangelical Protestantism, fundamentalist religions favor obedience to doctrine over independent thought. Many churches use martial language to promote a sense of siege that only obedient, disciplined soldiers can overcome. At its root, the political attack on gays rests on a narrow interpretation of a religious text. Since that condemnation coincides with already deeply held fears of difference, Bible-believing Christians have no reason to question it.

In Oklahoma as in Washington, D.C., elected officials only foment the demonization of gays while seeking the cover of biblical purity.

In Oklahoma unreflexive Christianity receives constant reinforcement. On evenings throughout the year, Oklahoma City's skyscrapers light office windows to form a cross on the sides of buildings. The state's largest newspaper includes a prayer on its front page every morning. Every spring students at my university host a well-publicized Jesus Week to spread the Gospel to their "lost" classmates. Promoting Christianity need not spread intolerance, but it normalizes belief based on faith, not evidence.

Christianity Is Used to Attack Gays

Increasingly Oklahomans use Christianity to justify attacks on gays. This year state legislators threatened to withhold financing from public libraries that did not relocate gay-themed children's books to the adult section. Again, supporters did not base their decision on evidence of actual harm inflicted on young readers from these books, but on an abiding conviction that homosexuality must be denounced.

This preference for prejudice over proof baffles my circle of friends at the university. We thumb copies of Thomas Frank's *What's the Matter with Kansas? How Conservatives Won the Heart of America* (Metropolitan Books, 2004) and George Lakott's *Don't Think of an Elephant! Know Your Values and Frame the Debate: The Essential Guide for Progressives* (Chelsea Green, 2004), seeking ways to frame our issues in a more palatable way. However, what these coastal thinkers miss is how Christianity saturates life here in a way unthinkable in California or New York. No clever argument in support of gay rights will silence the constant drumbeat of disapproval emanating from the churches.

Segregationists also used crude readings of the Bible to justify racist policies. Public protests helped win the last civil-rights struggle because courageous leaders valued careful thought over political expediency.

Like most biases, homophobia stems from unquestioned faith, not empirical knowledge.

Nowadays such valor is scarce. In Oklahoma as in Washington, D.C., elected officials only foment the demonization of gays while seeking the cover of biblical purity. Mr. Graves is no longer a state legislator, having served the maximum time allowed in that office, but his successors show the same willingness to let a homophobic Christianity guide their actions. And Mr. Graves has put himself on the ballot this fall as a candidate for district judge.

The Academic Bubble

Protected in my bubble, I did not perceive the connections between my sexuality and my academic role. By being outspoken about equality for gays and lesbians, I am not advancing a narrow personal interest; rather I am defending the fundamental principles of the university. Those principles promote intellectual conversation based on argument backed by evidence.

Claims without evidence, like those offered by Mr. Graves, impoverish the university because they forestall debate. How can I participate in a discussion over same-sex marriage or stem-cell research if the other side ignores my data? Like most biases, homophobia stems from unquestioned faith, not empirical knowledge. Sociological and cross-cultural studies counter every rational objection that opponents to same-sex marriage or parenting raise.

What's left is naked prejudice, a toxin that no state boundary can contain. To borrow the evangelicals' language, academic authority itself is under attack, and all scholars have a stake in defending it.

Homosexual Youths Are Proof that Gay Activism Has Succeeded

Ritch C. Savin-Williams

Ritch C. Savin-Williams is a professor of clinical and developmental psychology in human development at Cornell University in Ithaca, New York.

Derrick, a twenty-year-old college student from rural Ohio, came to discuss his career. I just assumed he was being gender-sensitive when he referred to his "partner" because nothing about Derrick or his mannerisms set off my gaydar. During our second discussion I inadvertently referred to his partner as a "she." Derrick looked bewildered. "Taylor is a *he*. We've been together for over a year." It was his response to my clumsy apology ("Sorry, I didn't realize you're gay") that became the inspiration for my book *The New Gay Teenager* (2005). Derrick, now bordering on annoyance, corrected me. "No, I'm not gay. I said Taylor is my partner." Derrick is not self-hating, homophobic, or confused about who he is. He just doesn't think he's gay.

Rejection of Gay Identity

Derrick is not a lone exception. This I discovered through interviewing young women with physical or romantic attractions to women, talking to youths in gay/straight alliances, reading youth stories gathered by others, listening to young people at the annual True Colors conference over the past decade, and reading the scientific literature. As teenagers with same-sex attractions become increasingly visible to themselves and to others, the desire to name their same-sex sexuality is

Ritch C. Savin-Williams, "The New Gay Teen: Shunning Labels," *The Gay and Lesbian Review*, vol. 12, no. 6, November 2005, pp. 16–19. www.glreview.com. Reproduced by permission.

waning. They might use "the gay word" as a shorthand method for describing their attractions, but implicit in this usage is a rejection of gay as an identity, much less as the defining characteristic of their sense of self.

But according to many gay-liberated adults of my generation, gay youths should loyally follow a hard-won script and be visible, political activists who fight for gay rights and denounce heterosexism and homophobia. After all, youths of all generations have endured ridicule because of their gender expression, can't openly date those they love most because same-sex romance in high school is still disparaged, and believe they must conceal their secret longings from parents and friends. Today's youth should appreciate all that my generation has done for them! Now it's their turn to assume the gay mantle, to take the lead in gay pride parades and to write the polemics denouncing integration into mainstream culture, conservative religious and political leaders, and materialism. To eschew these responsibilities is to betray generations of sexual and gender warriors.

Despite appearances their increasing failure to embrace activism is less a harbinger of the end of gay rights than a sign that gay activism has succeeded so well. Young people with same-sex attractions are now freer than ever to be themselves, comfortable with their sexuality, because they live in a youth culture that is increasingly nonchalant about diverse sexualities. This cohort believes that same-sex partners should have the option to marry, can't imagine that parents oppose gay teachers in their schools, and embraces media and marketing that explicitly portray same-sex lives and homoeroticism. In sum, they wish that their elders would just "get over it" and learn to treat all people with respect.

Gay Teens Are Not Defined by Their Sexuality

Two 21-year-old aspiring actors, Giovanni Andrade and Heather Matarazzo, are the beneficiaries of this new attitude.

Andrade doesn't like "the word *gay* because it's very restrictive. . . . But it's fair to say I'm gay because I have a boy-friend." Likewise, Matarazzo asserts that she doesn't want to be known "as a lesbian that happens to be an actress: I wanted to be known as an actress that happens to be with a woman. OK! Move on. Next subject."

They object to the gay label because they don't want their sexuality to define them. Perhaps in a similar way, eighteen-year-old Scott Williams of San Jose hopes that one day he will be accepted simply for who he is, and not as a stereotype. He's not one to run around "in a tight-fitting Abercrombie and Fitch T-shirt and designer sunglasses talking about last night's episode of *Queer Eye for the Straight Guy*. . . . It's as if I'm not straight enough or gay enough for the world." Not meeting the criteria for either category, he eschews labels altogether.

This failure of "gay" to fit the lives of young people is also reflected in the experience of nineteen-year-old Simone Sneed of Albany, N.Y. Coming out as a full-fledged lesbian when she was thirteen, she's now taking it back. Gay has become too va-nilla, irrelevant to her politics—the radical denunciation of hetero-normative culture. "Over the years I have met an ever-expanding population of queers, polyamorous people, flexuals, gender queers, bois, boy-girl wonders, tranny fags, tranny chasers, hetero boys who used to be lesbians, and lesbians who used to be hetero bio boys. . . . The gay community has bought into consumerism, and 'gay' no longer appears to be an iden-tity that my peers and I are comfortable with. . . . So please don't call me a lesbian."

Reasons for Rejecting Gay Identity

As these young adults testify, several motives drive the deci-sion to reject "gay" as an identity. Six of these are highlighted below. Our usual assumptions about youth who resist coming out as gay are that they can't (but want to) or that their self-loathing spawns denial.

1. *Safety.* Some youth fear the negative consequences of identifying as gay, especially if they live in secluded, conservative regions of the country. They might personally accept their sexuality but realize that it is unwise or imprudent to come out—at least until they are living among peers who accept diverse sexualities.

2. *Internalized homophobia.* Other youth, even those who live in relatively safe environments, are alienated, even disgusted, by the "unnaturalness" of their sexual attractions and the assumed inevitable gay lifestyle they would have to lead should they come out. These individuals are likely to be among the most violent gay-bashers and might remain closeted, perhaps forever.

For every high school student who identifies as gay, there are three, four, perhaps even ten others with same-sex attractions who do not.

Although it is uncertain as to whether youth in the above two categories constitute a majority or minority of those who reject identity labels, many other teenagers are motivated by reasons that seem uniquely modern:

3. *Fluidity.* For some youth, current same-sex attractions or relationships are considered discrete and imply nothing permanent about them, their sexuality, or their identity. They view their attractions as fluid beyond that which is permitted by sexual identity labels. It is the individual that attracts them, and should the relationship falter, the gender of their next lover might have no better than a fifty-fifty chance of being a same-sex partner. It is highly likely that reduced societal prejudice toward same-sex sexuality has contributed to the probability that these young people pursue sexual and romantic partners relatively independent of gender. Although this plas-

ticity often receives currency only among young women, I have met young men who are also sexually and romantically fluid.

4. *Philosophy.* Other young people fully embrace their same-sex orientation, but they philosophically oppose the relegation of their sexuality to an identity box. The mere creation of sexual categories reifies a label as an "it," a trait with stereotypical depictions that do not fit their experience. Labels are considered overly reductionist and unable to capture the full extent of their sexuality. Identity terms box them in, constrain their options, and over-simplify a complex aspect of the self. Their strongest preference is not to call their sexuality anything at all, not to compartmentalize their sexual desire, and not to link desire immediately with politics. Sex is about pleasure and happiness.

5. *Fit.* Despite the proliferation of gay media portraits, stereotypes linger. Many young people buy into these characterizations about what gays should value and how they should present themselves—and conclude, "This isn't me." In many cases, they object to the exaggerated, often comical, cross-gender representations. Butch males and femme females with same-sex attractions situate themselves here, but so too might youth who are neither particularly masculine nor feminine. Such youth are likely to be the majority of individuals with same-sex attractions.

6. *Politics.* Some youths oppose the political implications that are tied to a gay label. Two sorts comprise this group. First are those who assert that gay has become so mainstreamed, so "sold out," that they no longer wish to be associated with it. Their desire is to radically restructure modern sexuality discourse or to rebel for reasons other than their sexuality—perhaps to fight sexism, classism, or racism. Second are those who lament the equation of gay with "queer." The former has been shoved so far to the periphery of mainstream culture that "normal" youths such as themselves are excluded.

They're not sexual or political outlaws. so they're not gay—and don't want to be. In either case, they do not attribute the caricature of gayness to themselves.

Some Gays Embrace Their Identity

While several factors can inspire young people to reject a gay identity—and these may well change over time for one individual or across cohorts—it is clear that a significant number of same-sex-attracted young people do identify as gay, also for a variety of reasons: to right the wrongs of societal heterocentrism, to proclaim one's rebellion or political identity, to describe sexual preferences, to connect with like-minded others, to elicit help, or to solicit sex and/or love. Few of us object to their right to avow their gay status publicly: fewer still question whether this exhibitionism, as they see it, is ideal or necessary for all same-sex-attracted youth.

> *The jury is still out on what explains the mental health differences between gay and straight youth.*

Certainly, these self-identified gay youths are not in the majority among those with same-sex attractions. For every high school student who identifies as gay, there are three, four, perhaps even ten others with same-sex attractions who do not, whether privately or publicly. Surveys of adolescents across several countries (Australia, Britain, Japan, the Netherlands, New Zealand, Norway, Sweden, Switzerland, Turkey, and the U.S.) find that only two to three percent of adolescents identify as gay or have engaged in same-sex activities. However, admissions of same-sex sexual or romantic attractions are far larger, up to fifteen to twenty percent. Some of these youths may eventually adopt a gay or bisexual label, while others who currently identify as gay may subsequently de-identify once they tire of the label or no longer find it useful to gain a community, a lover, a connection.

Mental Health Concerns

Whether young people identify as gay directly affects estimates of their numbers, and thus the argument for attention and resources. Although such assessments are surely valuable, as a developmental and clinical psychologist, I am less interested in prevalence rates per se than in meaningful distinctions between those who do and do not identify as gay. For example, nearly all mental health research on same-sex-attracted youth is generated from the reports of self-identified gay youth, convincingly demonstrating that youths who identify as gay or engage in same-sex behavior are more likely than straight youths to be suicidal, depressed, anxious, distressed, victimized, and substance abusing. The resulting portrait is that of the "suffering suicidal" gay adolescent. This script is well known to most same-sex-attracted youths, informing them of how their life is likely to play out.

But does the script reflect their social reality? Research would suggest that to some extent it does. There are several possible explanations: 1) Gay-identified youth who participate in research are not representative of the larger population of same-sex-attracted youth; rather, whatever causes them to *identify* as gay is significantly related to mental health disturbance. 2) Gay youths over-report psychopathology, either because they believe they're supposed to fulfill the "suffering suicidal script" (that is, be a drama queen) or because they're more in touch with their inner self and hence small perturbations of psychological stability are noticed. 3) Gay youths are mentally disturbed because of their biology: that which makes them gay also creates mental health volatility (in biologic terms: "developmental instability" or "fluctuating asymmetry"). 4) Gay youths are mentally disturbed because of minority stress: adolescent clinical symptomatology results from unrelenting family, peer, and societal victimization and stigmatization, often from early childhood and often because of their gender-atypical behavior and interests—not because of their sexual orientation as such.

Gay Teens Feel Good About Themselves

The jury is still out on what explains the mental health differences between gay and straight youth. Regardless, some teens do not identify as gay because they've heard about the implied gay youth life trajectory and either fear its inevitability or fail to relate to it whatsoever. They are not experiencing meaningfully different life trajectories from those of their heterosexual peers, and it is this sense of sameness that drives them to want not to be different. This does not mean that they're uncomfortable with their sexuality, want to change it, or withhold information about it from others. Indeed, the vast majority of modern teens with same-sex attractions actually feel quite good about themselves. Levels of self-esteem do not differ from heterosexual peers, and most are not sitting around lamenting that they're gay. And, given a choice, most say they would not take a pill that would change their sexual orientation. Upwards of eighty percent reportedly feel "very good" or "okay" about their sexuality; only about five percent hate or would do anything to change their sexual orientation. Like their peers, they ruminate on love and romance, struggle to understand the conundrum known as parents, and wonder what they'll be when they grow up. Far down on their agenda is attempting suicide, abusing substances—or identifying as gay. To understand their lives, the best approach is not through the psychology of homosexuality but through that of basic adolescent development.

What this means for those of us who have spent our professional lives studying the plight of gay-identified youth is that we must stop treating them as if they were a separate species; stop focusing solely on "gay versus straight" research; stop directing attention only toward the liabilities while neglecting the assets of same-sex attraction; and stop treating them as if they were a collective, as if "gay youth" were a meaningful entity. If we allow same-sex-attracted youth to teach us anything, the current cohort instructs us to acknowledge their non-gay existence. New gay teenagers revel neither in the singularity nor the banality of same-sex attractions. Their desire is to witness the elimination of sexuality per se as the defining characteristic of the person. If achieved, gay identification would be relegated to an archaic memory, its social construct forgotten except as a historic footnote.

Big Business Is Gay Friendly

Marc Gunther

Marc Gunther is a senior writer at FORTUNE *magazine and a columnist at* CNNMoney.com

Business is booming at Raytheon, the $22-billion-a-year defense contractor that sells Tomahawk cruise missiles, laser-vision goggles and advanced radar systems to the Pentagon. This, improbably, is good news for the gay-rights movement.

A platoon of Raytheon employees wearing identical blue-and-black bowling shirts, pins with the company's logo, and black pants proudly walked the halls of this fall's convention of Out & Equal, an organization that brings together the networks of gay, lesbian, bisexual, and transgender people—GLBT, in the argot of the moment—that have taken root at America's big companies. For three days in Chicago, with about 1,700 delegates from other companies, the 67 members of Raytheon's GLBT network could attend workshops with such titles as "The Cost of Transgender Health Benefits," "Breaking Through the Lavender Ceiling," and "Male-on-Male Sexual Harassment: An Emerging Issue."

As a high-profile supporter of gay rights, Raytheon of course provides health-care benefits to the domestic partners of its gay employees. It does a lot more, too. The company supports a wide array of gay-rights groups, including the Human Rights Campaign, the nation's largest gay-advocacy group. Its employees march under the Raytheon banner at gay-pride celebrations and AIDS walks. And it belongs to gay chambers of commerce in communities where it has big plants. Why? you may ask. Not because gay people buy missiles or radar—at least as far as we know. No, it's because the competition to hire and retain engineers and other skilled

Marc Gunther, "Queer Inc.," *FORTUNE*, vol. 154, no. 12, December 11, 2006, p. 94.

workers is so brutal that Raytheon doesn't want to overlook anyone. To attract openly gay workers, who worry about discrimination, a company like Raytheon needs to hang out a big welcome sign. "Over the next ten years we're going to need anywhere from 30,000 to 40,000 new employees," explains Heyward Bell, Raytheon's chief diversity officer. "We can't afford to turn our back on anyone in the talent pool."

FORTUNE 500 Companies Support Gays

[Recently] the gay rights movement quietly achieved a milestone: For the first time, more than half of *FORTUNE* 500 companies—263 to be precise—offered health benefits for domestic partners, according to the Human Rights Campaign. Ten years ago only 28 did. Along with health benefits for their families, many workers also get bereavement leave when their same-sex partner dies, adoption assistance or paid leave if they have children, and relocation assistance for their partners if they are transferred. Put another way, gay marriage—an idea that has been banned by all but one of 27 states that have voted on it—has become a fact of life inside many big companies.

People who once were shunned and then merely tolerated are today being embraced by corporate America.

"Corporate America is far ahead of America generally when it comes to the question of equality for GLBT people," says Joe Solmonese, president of the Human Rights Campaign.

Solmonese is right. The nation's Roman Catholic bishops last month advised gays to be celibate because the church considers their sexuality "disordered." Prominent evangelical minister Ted Haggard stepped down from his church after he was accused of getting massages from a gay man. Social conservatives flock to the polls to oppose gay marriage.

Business is different. "It's not a faith-based community," says Ed Offshack, a chemical engineer and gay activist at Procter & Gamble. "It's a logic-based community." The changes in attitudes toward gays and lesbians have been swift, deep, and altogether remarkable. People who once were shunned and then merely tolerated are today being embraced by corporate America. Yes, embraced. And not just on Seventh Avenue and in Hollywood.

When Justin Nelson was trying to get the National Gay and Lesbian Chamber of Commerce off the ground in 2003, IBM offered its support. "If they hadn't joined, there wouldn't be a chamber," Nelson says. Big Blue was followed by Wells Fargo, Motorola, Intel, American Express, and recently, Wal-Mart. Today the Washington-based gay chamber, which has 24,000 members, certifies small businesses as gay-owned so that they can qualify for supplier-diversity programs at big companies. Think about that: Homosexuality, once a career-killing secret, has become enough of a competitive advantage in some circles that certification is needed to deter straight people from passing as gay.

Companies are taking their support for gay rights into the political arena. Last spring, after internal soul-searching, Microsoft was persuaded by its GLBT employee group, GLEAM (Gay and Lesbian Employees at Microsoft) to support state legislation to ban discrimination against gays. CEO Steve Ballmer said, "Diversity in the workplace is such an important issue for our business that it should be included in our legislative agenda."

Yes, the world of work is changing—though not without a backlash.

Some companies are grappling with how to manage employees switching from one sex to another. American Airlines and its HR people helped a 58-year-old pilot—an ex-Marine and Vietnam combat veteran—go from being Robert to Bobbi. Energy giant Chevron published "Transgender@Chevron," an eight-page guide to the issues that come up when a worker changes gender identity, ranging from the bureaucratic (don't forget to get a new security badge) to the everyday (when it's appropriate to move from the men's room to the ladies' room or vice versa).

Progressive Companies Face Backlash

Yes, the world of work is changing—though not without a backlash.

When Walgreens, Kraft, and Harris Bank signed up to sponsor the 2006 Gay Games, a weeklong festival in Chicago that attracted 11,000 athletes, conservative Christian groups attacked. Peter LaBarbera, the president of Americans for Truth, which calls itself the only national organization devoted exclusively to exposing and countering the homosexual activist agenda, wrote to Walgreens: "Make no mistake: The 'Gay Games' was conceived as a way to build acceptance for homosexuality in the name of sport—a perversion of the athletic ideal." A Walgreens' store manager in Alabama quit in protest. Chief executive David Bernauer got 250,000 e-mails, most from a website of the American Family Association, another Christian group. "Having the CEO's server crash was not a positive thing," says Phil Burgess, national director of pharmacy operations at Walgreens. Burgess, who is gay, said the company made the $100,000 donation to support its GLBT employees and let gay and lesbian customers know that they are welcome at Walgreens. The company writes more prescriptions for AIDS-related drugs than any other pharmacy chain.

Some people may simply wish all the controversy would go away. "It's a distraction," says Stephen Viscusi, the (gay) owner of an executive-search firm. "You should be defined by the work you do." People can do whatever they want in bed, this line of thinking goes, but in the workplace, sexual orientation shouldn't matter.

The trouble is, it still does: In 34 states it's legal to fire an employee simply for being gay. Last winter a photographer named Laurel Scherer, who took pictures of skiers at the Wolf Laurel Ski Area near Asheville, N.C., lost her contract with the resort after she and her partner were married in Massachusetts and ran their wedding announcement in the Asheville Citizen Times. The Human Rights Campaign gets about 25 to 30 complaints a month about workplace discrimination.

Corporate Changes Happen from the Inside Out

What would people think? Mike Syers, a 42-year-old partner at Ernst & Young, was coming out in a very big way. About 3,000 partners of the firm had gathered in Orlando for a conference last year. A two-minute video of Syers played on giant TV screens throughout the convention center. He sat in the audience watching himself.

This is how workplace changes typically happen at big companies—from the inside out.

"When I started in public accounting," the onscreen Syers said, "I really didn't think there was a long-term career opportunity for me. Being a gay man, I didn't see gay partners." But things were different at E&Y, he said. He felt comfortable and welcomed.

As the screen went dark, Syers's BlackBerry began vibrating. Messages of support poured in. Afterward a partner came up to him to say that his son was gay, and that he would call home that night to tell his son how proud he was to work at E&Y.

E&Y had asked Syers to make the video because he is a leader of bEYond, the company's GLBT employee group. bEYond is only two years old, but it sent 72 people to this fall's Out & Equal convention. It also sponsored the 2006 Reaching Out MBA conference, a gay and lesbian recruiting event that attracted about 700 MBA students to New York. Courting them were Accenture, Dell, Goldman Sachs, J.P. Morgan Chase, Lehman Bros., McKinsey, Merrill Lynch, Microsoft, Target, and Toyota, among others.

This is how workplace changes typically happen at big companies—from the inside out. Gay and lesbian employees come out of the closet. They find one another. They organize. They enlist straight allies. And they take their concerns to top managers.

The first company-sanctioned network of gays, called League, was formed by gay employees at AT&T in 1987. Now more than 110 company-supported GLBT employee groups have registered with Out & Equal. . . .

Businesses Market to Gay Consumers

Mainstream marketers are getting comfortable tailoring their messages to brand-savvy GLBT customers.

---

175 FORTUNE *500 companies run advertisements or websites aimed at gay consumers.*

"Whether you're planning to spend Gay Ski Week in Whistler with your friends or to take your partner to Boston so you can hop over to Provincetown to enjoy Lesbian Week, we have terrific options for you."

So goes the pitch at AAVacations.com/rainbow, American Airlines' website for gay and lesbian travelers. The website features a list of gay-friendly destinations and a calendar of gay-related events (Mid-Atlantic Leather Weekend, Sydney Gay and Lesbian Mardi Gras) along with the boast that American is the only airline to score a perfect 100% on the Human Rights Campaign's Corporate Equality Index for the past four years.

American is one of about 175 *FORTUNE* 500 companies that run advertisements or websites aimed at gay consumers. Gay buying power is estimated to be $641 billion in 2006, according to Bob Witeck and Wes Combs, authors of Business Inside Out: Capturing Millions of Brand Loyal Gay Consumers. They argue that companies need to be gay-friendly in all respects to win over GLBT customers.

CHAPTER 3

Should Society Encourage Increased Acceptance of Homosexuality?

Chapter Preface

Perhaps one reason why American society has grown more accepting of gays and lesbians is that there is a perception that greater numbers of homosexuals are in the political mainstream. Gays and lesbians are no longer automatically assumed to be leftist radicals and progressive stalwarts of the Democratic Party. Contrary to the political Left's attempt to corner the market on gay authenticity, a substantial number of homosexuals identify with and are members of the Republican Party. In 2000, 25 percent of gay voters cast ballots for George W. Bush. Four years later, according to Rich Tafel, an ordained Baptist minister, graduate of Harvard Divinity School, and former executive director of the Log Cabin Republicans, a national gay and lesbian Republican grassroots organization, the president received anywhere from 1.5 million to 2 million gay votes. This represents an increase of 1 million votes from four years prior and double the number of gay votes garnered by Republican presidential candidate Bob Dole in 1996. This growing gay and lesbian support was despite the facts that Log Cabin Republicans, for the first time since the founding of their organization in 1993, did not endorse the Republican presidential candidate and that President Bush supported a constitutional amendment to bar same-sex couples from marrying. Rising gay and lesbian preferences for Republican candidates is also evident by the increase in Log Cabin chapters, particularly in GOP-dominated Southern states. From 2003 to 2007, the number of recognized Log Cabin chapters has tripled to over 85. Total membership has increased almost five-fold, growing from 3,750 in December 2002 to 18,462 in October 2005. Moreover, the organization's annual budget has mushroomed 400 percent to $1 million from 2002 to 2006.

This dramatic increase in gay and lesbian political support for Republicans in 2004 was partly an indication that many gays, not unlike many heterosexuals, have strong libertarian leanings. They embrace GOP opposition to welfare and affirmative action and support the party's stances in favor of limited government, personal responsibility, individual rights, and low taxes. Another reason was President George W. Bush's commitment to a strong national defense. The Log Cabin Republicans argue that more and more gays and lesbians are putting group interest concerns like gay marriage and gay adoption aside and are acknowledging that the rise of militant and homophobic Islam is a real and fatal threat. Seeing how their brothers and sisters are physically abused in the predominately Muslim countries, gays and lesbians realize that they have a great stake in the War on Terror and the total defeat of the worldwide "jihadi" movement. As a consequence, many homosexuals have more faith that Republicans will press forward and defeat the enemy. In contrast, many gays and lesbians see the Democratic Party as too dovish and criticize them for viewing terrorism as a law enforcement problem instead of a military one.

Despite the growing rapprochement between the Republican Party and homosexuals, there remain fundamental splits between the latter and the Christian Right, an influential coalition within the party. For example, the vast majority of gays and lesbians believe that homosexual families deserve the same rights, benefits, and responsibilities as all other American families. These rights include gay adoption and civil marriage. Political scientists believe that a key reason why Republicans lost the Congressional majority in 2006 was because the party alienated independent voters. Exit polls show that independents, in a sharp turn-about from the 2004 election, favored Democrats over Republicans 57 percent to 39 percent. While some voter disaffection was certainly due to ongoing problems in the execution of the War on Terror, gay and lesbian Republicans also blame congressional losses on the Christian Right. For example, the Christian Coalition of America, the largest and most active conservative grassroots organization in the nation, and the Traditional Values Coalition, which represents over 43,000 conservative Christian churches in the United States, are strongly opposed to homosexuality and the lesbian, gay, bisexual, and transgender rights movement. Log Cabin Republicans are attempting to stem the loss of independents in 2008 by denouncing what they deem the Christian Right's advocacy of "discrimination, bigotry, and fear of homosexuals" and championing a more diverse and inclusive GOP.

Gay Professional Athletes Should Not Have to Fear Being Outed

L. Jon Wertheim

L. Jon Wertheim is a senior writer for Sports Illustrated.

A round the same time that Magic Johnson disclosed that he had HIV, a far less luminous star in the NBA cosmos gave thought to disclosing that he was gay. He decided that lugging around the secret of his "lifestyle" like a spare tire was, finally, less burdensome than facing the consequences of revealing it. A friend of the player's told SI that the potential for disrupting that ineffable, all-important team chemistry figured into the decision. But the most important factor was the fans' potential reaction. "He had visions of getting booed when he touched the ball and being subjected to slurs every night," says the friend. "And the road games would have been worse."

That was in the early 1990s. In the decade since, attitudes toward homosexuality in sports have ... well, it's hard to say what they've done. In response to the buzz created at the Sundance Film Festival by *Ring Fire*, the documentary about Emile Griffith, and in anticipation of its telecast on April 20, NBC and USA Network commissioned a national poll last month on the issue of homosexuality in sports. Responses reveal that the subject not only cleaves public opinion—which, of course, was already known by folks on both sides of the red state–blue state division—but is also a source of deep conflict for individual respondents.

"Gays in Sports: A Poll; Americans Believe They Have Become More Accepting—But Have They?" *Sports Illustrated*, vol. 102, no. 16, April 18, 2005. Copyright © 2005 Time, Inc. Reproduced by permission.

No Major Professional Athlete Is Openly Gay

Consider that of 979 people interviewed, 86% agreed that it is O.K. for male athletes to participate in sports, even if they are openly gay, yet nearly a quarter of the respondents agreed that having an openly gay player hurts the entire team. "It was like, I'm O.K. with this, but if you press me, I have some doubts," says Doug Schoen, whose firm, Penn, Schoen & Berland Associates, conducted the poll.

In the face of such data it comes as no great shock that while homosexuals are thought to compose anywhere from 4% to 10% of the general population, among the 3,500 or so men active in the four major professional sports not a single homosexual is "out." The few pro athletes who have divulged their homosexuality have, tellingly, done so in retirement, long after they depended on teammates to pass them the ball or execute a block and long after they depended on fans to, effectively, pay their salaries. The gay lifestyle may be increasingly accepted—embraced even—in a mainstream popular culture that beams *Will & Grace's* Jack McFarland and a not-that-there's-anything-wrong-with-it ethos into our living rooms. But in a sports culture that hemorrhages testosterone and is widely read as a barometer of machismo, homosexuality remains the love that dares not speak its name.

Hostility Toward Gays

Examples of athletes showing hostility toward gays are many and varied, from [former Denver Broncos] running back Garrison Hearst's declaring, "I don't want any faggots on my team" to [NBA player] Allen Iverson's rapping about "faggot tendencies" to [former NFL wide receiver] Sterling Sharpe's telling HBO that his former Seattle Seahawks teammate Esera Tuaolo was wise to have concealed his homosexuality while he was an active player. "Had he come out on a Monday, with

Wednesday, Thursday and Friday practices, he'd have never gotten to the other team," Sharpe said.

Compounding the dilemma of a gay athlete is the virtual certainty that the first active player to come out will do so at his financial peril.

Even professed tolerance can be revealing. During his disastrous appearance before Congress last month, [baseball player] Mark McGwire read a statement claiming, "I do not sit in judgment of other players, whether it deals with their sexual preference, their marital problems . . . including whether or not they use chemical substances." McGwire clearly meant to convey open-mindedness, but it did not go unnoticed that he grouped sexual preference with ills on the order of domestic strife and drug use.

Says Giants pitcher Jason Christiansen, who says he has a gay relative, "I don't think attitudes of ballplayers have changed over the years."

Openly Gays Might Face Economic Backlash

Compounding the dilemma of a gay athlete is the virtual certainty that the first active player to come out will do so at his financial peril. Those Red Sox fans clad in shirts reading JETER'S A HOMO and those NASCAR gearheads who frequent the website—note the acronym—Fans Against Gordon are also consumers. According to Schoen's poll 18% of Americans would be less likely to purchase footwear or apparel endorsed by a gay athlete. (Roughly 4% would be more likely.) "If I were a marketer looking at this data," says Schoen, "I would say, 'Boy, if I have an openly gay athlete, I may well have problems I don't need.'"

Adds Dean Bonham, a Denver-based sports-marketing expert, "The question isn't whether coming out would have a negative impact on an athlete as an endorser. The question is, how much of a negative impact."

With that as a backdrop, it's no wonder that Kordell Stewart, when he was a Pittsburgh Steelers quarterback, called a team meeting to scuttle rumors that he was gay. ("You'd better not leave your girlfriends around me," he allegedly warned, "because I'm out to prove a point!") Or that, in a truly postmodern moment, [baseball catcher] Mike Piazza called an impromptu press conference to announce defiantly, "I date women." Or that, after it came to light that he had appeared in a gay porn video, Indians minor league pitcher Kazuhito Tadano tearfully apologized but insisted, "I'm not gay. I'd like to clear that fact up right now."

Attitudes May Be Changing

The wheels of change may spin slowly in sports, but they do spin. A full 79% of the poll respondents agreed that Americans are more accepting of gays in sports today than they were 20 years ago. Reality bears this out. Owing to her status as an avowed lesbian, Martina Navratilova was commercially radioactive in the 1980s, when she was the best tennis player in the world; she now endorses products from Under Armour to Juiceman. During spring training Johnny Damon, Tim Wakefield and three other Boston Red Sox players taped a segment of *Queer Eye for the Straight Guy*, replete with back waxings and spa treatments. (Maybe it's not the most compelling evidence of a cultural shift, but try for a second to imagine [baseball player] Ted Williams submitting to an afternoon with [*Queer Eye* star] Carson Kressley and the gang.) Asked last week whether he would accept a gay teammate, Ken Griffey Jr. laughed and said, "Wouldn't bother me at all. If you can play, you can play." Who knows? With attitudes like Griffey's, there will come a day when locker rooms and clubhouses cease to double as walk-in closets. But as Schoen's poll confirms, we're not there yet.

The American Episcopal Church Rightfully Ordains Homosexual Clergy

Barry Jay Seltser

Barry Jay Seltser has a PhD in religious studies and sociology from Yale University in New Haven, Connecticut.

Many Roman Catholics, ordained and lay, were understandably concerned when the Vatican issued its statement last fall barring men with "deep-seated homosexual tendencies" from the priesthood. If a priest is faithful to his promise of chaste celibacy, what difference does it make if he understands himself to be homosexual? Many people thought it was celibacy, not sexual orientation, that mattered when it came to priestly discipline.

I share the feeling of many people in thinking it is unjust to bar celibate homosexuals from the priesthood. But Rome may have had multiple reasons for issuing such a divisive instruction. Among those possible reasons is the way in which the debate over homosexuality, and especially over the influence, status, and authority of homosexual priests and ministers, has roiled nearly every Protestant denomination. Most conspicuous among those churches where attitudes toward homosexuality pose a serious threat to ecclesial unity is the Anglican Communion.

Anglican Schism Is Possible

At its 2003 General Convention, the Episcopal Church of the United States of America (ECUSA) voted to approve the consecration of Gene Robinson, an active homosexual living in a

Barry Jay Seltser, "Episcopalian Crisis: Authority, Homosexuality & the Future of Anglicanism," *Commonweal*, vol. 133, no. 10, May 19, 2006, pp. 11–16. Copyright © 2006 Commonweal Publishing Co., Inc. Reproduced by permission of Commonweal Foundation.

committed relationship, as bishop of New Hampshire. At the same time, the Anglican Church of Canada authorized the blessing of same-sex unions. A firestorm erupted, both in North America and worldwide across the Anglican Communion of thirty-eight loosely allied national and regional churches. Conservative and evangelical Episcopalians, especially Anglican primates in Africa, Asia, and South America, made their outrage and objections known in no uncertain terms. Many threatened to leave the Anglican Communion if Robinson's ordination stood, or to try to exclude the American Episcopal Church from the Communion.

The archbishop of Canterbury, Rowan Williams, who is the symbolic head of the Anglican Communion, sought to forestall outright schism. Williams, believed to be personally sympathetic to the ordination of homosexuals, urged caution on the ECUSA. He commissioned "The Windsor Report," released in 2004, which urged the ECUSA to apologize for its actions and to embrace a moratorium on ordaining openly gay bishops and blessing same-sex unions. As Williams recently told the interviewer David Frost, changing church teaching and practice about homosexuality is not a step any one church in the Anglican Communion should undertake on its own. "For a change on that," Williams said, "I think we would need, as a Communion, to have a far greater level of consensus than we in fact have. Which is why the American determination to go it alone is worrying."

The Episcopal Church is democratic and pluralistic in its rules and decision making, and the authority vested in any individual or role is severely limited.

The forging of any broader consensus on the question of homosexuality seems unlikely. Whether American Episcopalians are determined to go it alone is likely to be decided at their next general convention, to be held in Columbus, Ohio,

June 13-21 [2006]. At the top of the convention's agenda may be the approval of another openly gay bishop. Liberal and conservative groups are already maneuvering to contest the disposition of church property if conservative Episcopal churches, and even dioceses, consequently leave the ECUSA and affiliate themselves with dioceses in Africa and elsewhere, as some already have. Few observers think the predominantly liberal ECUSA will back away from the ordination of more open or sexually active gay bishops, which many Episcopalians see as the logical extension of a struggle for equal rights that first led to the still contested ordination of women as priests and bishops. The Anglican Church in England, for example, although it ordains women as priests, has not yet, out of a concern for ecclesial unity, ordained a woman as bishop.

Looking at the impending implosion of the Anglican Communion, Rome, from its perspective, is perhaps more forward thinking than its critics suspect in trying to forestall any similar battle in the Catholic Church. Catholics who hope their church will change its teaching about homosexuality, the ordination of women, priestly celibacy and marriage, and contraception, while adopting a more collegial approach to the exercise of authority and greater respect for individual conscience, should be chastened by the current crisis in the Episcopal Church. As an Episcopalian who supports and is thankful for his church's progressive stances on all these issues, I am nevertheless concerned about the health and integrity of my church.

The Episcopalian Church Is a Democratic Institution

Situating the ECUSA in the larger Anglican Communion is tricky. Without denying the sense of commonality with the rest of the Anglican churches, I suspect that most American Episcopalians could imagine themselves as a completely separate church, cut off from communion with the other Anglican churches, much more easily than Roman Catholics could think of themselves as a separate national church. As a result, the ECUSA is much freer to adopt changes and move in different directions even if it risks being out of step—and even out of communion—with more traditional members of its international fellowship. For Episcopalians, it may be easier to hold divergent views because there is seldom one official position or central authority to enforce the "orthodox" position. The Episcopal Church is democratic and pluralistic in its rules and decision making, and the authority vested in any individual or role is severely limited. General Conventions are held every three years, with clergy and lay participants being elected to the House of Deputies, and bishops meeting as the House of Bishops. The Episcopal Church mirrors the American political system in many respects; local dioceses, functioning with significant autonomy, elect their own bishops in a local convention representing lay and ordained members, and the decision must then be ratified by a national vote.

The current situation with regard to gay bishops who are sexually active is a "perfect storm."

Episcopalian bishops have a form of authority that is much closer to what sociologists would call "influence" than "power." The local parish selects its priest, with the bishop's approval; bishops can help shape priorities but are usually unsuccessful if they move too far ahead of their parishes. Each diocese selects its own bishop, subject to the approval of a national convention. There is a presiding bishop of the U.S. church, and the archbishop of Canterbury is the most preeminent figure in the international Anglican Communion, but any suggestion that either of these figures approaches the pope in terms of power or even influence would be met with hilarious laughter.

The Perfect Storm

For several reasons, the current situation with regard to gay bishops who are sexually active is a "perfect storm." First, while liberal and conservative positions have long coexisted within the Episcopal Church and the Anglican Communion, the ordination of Bishop Robinson leaves less room for compromise than many earlier disputes. Bishops baptize, confirm, ordain other priests, and lay on their hands at the consecration of other bishops. Although their power is greatly attenuated by a church polity that mirrors, and in fact owes much of its design to, the American distrust of centralized authority, bishops are the key representatives of the local church. Still, an "illegitimate" bishop affects not only one diocese but the integrity of the entire religious community.

Second, the issue of homosexuality seems to present a stark contrast between different approaches to authority, and particularly to the role of the Bible in decision making. Although different approaches to Scripture can be finessed or compromised on many issues (such as the role of women in the church or the appropriate understanding of the Eucharist), conflict over the appropriateness of homosexual relationships is hard to avoid. A significant number of Episcopalians read Scripture quite literally, and insist that there is no appeal where Scripture speaks plainly and with one voice. Several biblical passages that appear to condemn homosexual behavior (at least for males) are regarded as determinative, especially when there are no corresponding passages that support homosexuality. To claim that the Bible allows homosexual behavior, or to ignore apparently clear statements of biblical morality, threatens the center of the community's loyalty and adherence to the Word of God through the revelatory text.

On the other side, many Episcopalians insist that the specific words of Scripture must be placed in the context of broader historical or literary interpretation, current understandings of the nature of homosexuality, or the witness of Christians living in faithful relationships with a member of the same sex. Liberals argue either that Scripture, properly interpreted, allows room for a variety of sexual practices or norms, or that even if Scripture speaks unequivocally about sexual ethics, its guidance is not necessarily the final word for the church today. The more significant theological split is occasioned by the latter approach, which challenges not only a particular understanding of scriptural texts but the very authority of Scripture itself. The gap between the more conservative and more liberal perspectives is enormous, with little apparent middle ground.

The conflict over homosexuality frequently reveals a deep visceral distaste, even disgust, for the behaviors under consideration.

Third, as in the Roman Catholic Church, the Episcopal Church is increasingly polarized along ideological lines. Theological or social disputes are seen in the context of the ongoing "culture wars" that seem to pit religious Americans against "secularists." The political battles of the past decade and the media obsession with finding and reinforcing opposing views make compromise even harder. It is not surprising that people who read the newspapers and watch television talking heads who take extreme views on the issues of the day will be likely to carry such attitudes about conflict into their activities in their parishes and dioceses.

Finally, I think that while it is seldom acknowledged, the conflict over homosexuality frequently reveals a deep visceral distaste, even disgust, for the behaviors under consideration. Many other biblical prohibitions—against divorce, women speaking in church, eating certain foods—have been altered. People may oppose the practice of ordaining women or consecrating them as bishops, but few appear to be physically disgusted by the prospect. The apparently unequivocal nature of the condemnations of homosexuality found in the Bible is reinforced by the deeper "instinctive" conviction that homosexual behavior simply cannot be what God intends for his creation. And for those on the liberal side (where I am), there is often a similar, almost visceral, reaction that sees opponents as simply intolerant and homophobic.

Can Episcopalians Resolve Their Differences?

Some of the debate in the Episcopal Church also focuses on process, on what Rowan Williams called the ECUSA's "determination to go it alone." Conservatives point to earlier pronouncements by the Anglican Communion saying the church was not ready to move ahead on this issue, and accuse the Americans of riding roughshod over both the precedents of the community and the feelings of other churches. Liberals insist that they have followed the established procedure for selecting and consecrating a bishop by receiving the required number of votes at both diocesan and national meetings, and that local dioceses and national churches have the right to take such steps.

Both sides may be narrowly correct but both are broadly misleading in their complaints about due process. It is hard to believe that opponents of Bishop Robinson's consecration would have been less opposed if the church had delayed and tried to convince others of the rightness of this step. One noted conservative voice makes this clear when he writes that this is a "subject on which Bible Christians are not able to change their minds. Not because we are dinosaurs—but because we believe God has already spoken." And on the other side, organizational autonomy and responsibility within a religious communion must mean more than simply justifying one's actions on the basis of what the official policies allow one to do.

Given these disagreements, how can Episcopalians resolve their differences? Do we remain within an institution that appears to be falling apart, and one that each side experiences as betraying our own commitment to theological orthodoxy or fairness? As a heterosexual who does not view homosexuality as intrinsically sinful or abnormal, can I continue to value the orthodox tradition that is part of my religious identity within a polity that seems so confused about what the "Christian" church should do?

I remain within the Episcopalian Church in part because I want to be a member of a community that allows for diverse views and alternative interpretations.

I know many Catholics ask the same questions about their church's teachings on contraception and other disputed issues. Autobiography is crucial here. My own views are shaped in part by the Jewish tradition I lived in for most of my life, before I became a Christian sixteen years ago. As I experienced and loved it, Judaism is a tradition steeped in a text but also committed at its core to interpretation and adaptation. The structure of the key Jewish sources through which the Bible is read is inherently dialogical; rabbinic figures debate with one another over the meaning of particular biblical verses, citing alternative verses or different meanings of the same words, different analogies, or diverse human experiences. The goal is seldom theoretical understanding for its own sake, but rather practical understanding to allow the community to remain faithful to a long-standing covenant while living in very different historical circumstances. The Jewish tradition has its own liberal/conservative continuum, but the center of the tradition is one of a continually changing and creative interaction of a community with its authorizing texts. This set of experiences and my personal commitment to open intellectual discussion and debate leave me very uncomfortable with the idea that specific biblical passages are always the determining or sole source of divine guidance or inspiration. . . .

I Will Not Leave the Church

I remain within the Episcopal Church in part because I want to be a member of a community that allows for diverse views and alternative interpretations, views that force me, along with others in my community, to struggle with what we think God is doing. I would rather be part of a church whose conservatives force me to be informed and guided by Scripture, even when I am inclined to dismiss what seem like anachronistic and even unjust teachings. And I would rather be part of a church whose liberals force me to listen to new voices and perspectives, even when I am inclined to dismiss them as modernist, unorthodox, or faddish.

To my mind, the question of whether an openly and sexually actively gay person can serve as a bishop is not a matter of essential Christian faith, nor is the identity or faithfulness of Episcopalians threatened by such service. I respect those who feel differently, but I think they are confusing the essential with the inessential. I believe the identity and faithfulness of the church are threatened far more by those who think the Gnostic Gospels or *The Da Vinci Code* has more to teach us than the Nicene Creed or the central texts of the Bible. I wish the ECUSA had waited a bit longer to take the step to ordain a sexually active homosexual person as bishop, and I wish the opponents of that step were more willing to consider whether God may be doing something new in our own time. But I continue to be an Episcopalian because the arguments, the disagreements, and even the threats of schism are all part of a messy and all-too-human way of struggling together to glimpse the nature and actions of an ultimately unknowable and infinitely loving God.

A Queer-Inclusive Curriculum Should Be Taught in English Classes

Mollie V. Blackburn and J.F. Buckley

Mollie V. Blackburn teaches at Ohio State University in Columbus and J.F. Buckley teaches at Ohio State University's Mansfield campus.

To a lesbian professor working with graduate students in education, and a gay professor working with undergraduate students in English (the authors); or to any educator working for social and cultural change, it is not news that U.S. public high schools are generally heterosexist, often homophobic institutions that tend to foster an irrational fear of lesbian, gay, bisexual, transgender, and questioning people (LGBTQ). Even when they provide for physical safety and espouse respect for diversity, few secondary schools advocate studying literature that addresses sexual diversity. The English language arts (ELA) curricula in U.S. public high schools often either ignore or reject the connection between same-sex desire and literature. ELA curricula are not, in other words, "queer inclusive."

Queer Theory Confronts Bigotry

We deliberately argue for queer-inclusive curricula rather than LGBTQ-inclusive curricula. An LGBTQ-inclusive curriculum would expose students to certain authors and texts, but a queer-inclusive curriculum would educate students about the interconnections among sexuality, identity, and literature. According to queer theorists, queer is not the lumping together of lesbian, gay, bisexual, and transgender, although it does pay particular attention to sexual and gender identities such as these. Rather, queer is the suspension of these classification. Queer theorists recognize sexual and gender identities as social, multiple, variable, shifting, and fluid; and while they allow for movement among such identity categories, they advocate for movement outside of these categories as well. For example, queer theorists not only allow for movement from bisexual to lesbian, but also from lesbian to straight; furthermore, they allow for the suspension of such categorization entirely. By rejecting categories of identity, queer theorists interrogate and disrupt notions of normal, not only with particular respect to sexuality and gender, but also with respect to race and class identities. Thus, queer theory works against the oppression that comes with being named, labeled, and tagged—an oppression that LGBTQ youth experience all too often in schools.

Academics Are Hindered by Heterosexism and Homophobia

A part of teaching is understanding that LGBTQ youth need to form their own school clubs, such as Gay Straight Alliances (GSAs), and to attend proms with same-sex dates. However, we believe it to be more important that high school students examine their cultural connections to what they study. As it is, most LGBTQ students in ELA find themselves learning how to recognize, value, and accumulate knowledge that locates them as outsiders and most of their classmates as insiders. Their academic learning—the reason they are in school—is hindered by heterosexism and homophobia: [E.C.] Goldblatt, for example, found that "a gap between private and public self creates an inhospitable climate for writing. . . . Writers who are alienated from or insecure within the institutional framework of their writing task will predictably have trouble composing texts for that institution."

Not much has changed. When Buckley (second author), as a gay teen, was introduced to Ernest Hemingway's *The Sun Also Rises*, his teacher would not entertain his suggestion that Jake Barnes might be campily dismissing Brett Ashley's belief in a future "good time together," not because of a war wound but because of conflicted sexuality. As a high school senior, Blackburn (first author) identified a research topic by selecting Edward Field from a list of poets distributed by her English teacher. In her research she discovered that Field was gay. As a consequence, she was more engaged in the project. However, she earned a poor grade because she included biographical information about the author's sexuality, which, she was told, was irrelevant and inappropriate.

By learning about LGBTQ persons and issues, students are given opportunities to surrender some of their hate.

Students Need to Surrender Hate

Given that the institutional framework of high school ELA consciously and publicly silences certain sexualities, straight or "normal" students also suffer pedagogically. When the literature that tells LGBTQ stories is excluded from curricula, all students learn is that "those people" do nothing worth mentioning. Conversely, by learning about LGBTQ persons and issues, students are given opportunities to surrender some of their hate. This is significant because "[h]ate is a debilitating burden to carry around; letting go of oppression, on the other hand, allows a stunted mind to grow to a more inclusive understanding of the human experience." At the very least, homopbobic students are forced to intellectually engage with mores and values and people they feel unable to accept socially. Without queer-inclusive ELA curricula that include the scope of human experience, the study of literature is myopic and reduces learning to an artificially "'focused gathering'—a set of persons engrossed in a common flow of activity and relating to one another in terms of that flow." Wisdom, however, reaches beyond the common flow and comes from ELA curricula that acknowledge, and then work against, the tendency of any perspective to position people as either insiders or outsiders in exaggerated social dichotomies where differences are emphasized at the expense of similarities:

> Not only does wisdom avoid adopting a position that is either for or against and entering into an antagonistic relationship, but, furthermore, it corresponds to every position, depending on the circumstances, placing them all on equal footing. . . . Wisdom is comprehensive and right from the start encompasses opposed points of view.

The Civil Rights Movement Should Include Gays

Consider that learning about the U.S. Civil Rights movement, in most curricula, starts with the Montgomery (Alabama) bus boycott of December 1, 1955, and ends approximately with the march from Selma to Montgomery on March 25, 1965, and the Voting Rights Act of that same year. Not that schools consider racial equality to follow immediately on the heels of Reverend King's march; rather, that after the notoriety of the church bombing on "Bloody Sunday," the country was ready for the changes that signaled the end of one era and the start of another. However, the era of protest was not over. The drag queens who resisted discrimination and police violence at New York City's Stonewall Inn on June 27, 1969, are not seen as related to the Civil Rights movement, even though, for some of them, their race, perhaps as much as their sexuality, made them targets of discrimination and hatred. It is sad that students do not learn how the speeches and literature of the Civil Rights movement were a catalyst for America's gay rights movement, a movement that, in its early years, nonetheless became mostly white, middle class, and male. Furthermore, students do not learn that the 1963 march on Washington, in which Dr. Martin Luther King, Jr., delivered his famous "I Have a Dream" speech, was planned and directed by Bayard Rustin, a gay African American whom Reverend King defended even though some in the movement thought him a liability.

Discussions of same-sex desire need to be incorporated into larger discussions of diversity.

Queer-inclusive Curricula Benefits All Students

To avoid perpetuating such a state of affairs, we believe that teachers need to construct ELA curricula that reveal the LGBTQ presence in all of our lives, and be aware that heterosexuality is assumed, and homosexuality and bisexuality are often ignored, in contemporary culture. We believe that teachers must be able to talk about LGBTQ persons and issues without "embarrassment or condemnation." They need to discuss the awkward, the different, and the new so that all students get opportunities to learn about the range of gender and sexual identities that constitute everyone's world. That is, we want educators to develop ELA curricula that include many perspectives, curricula that include such books as *The House You Pass on the Way*, which couches its treatment of gay rights in larger discussions of the Civil Rights movement. We believe high school ELA teachers need to disrupt the notion that being LGBTQ is some sort of poor, evil choice to work against the abuse and neglect that many LGBTQ students, and those perceived as such, experience. Queer-inclusive curricula benefit all students. Wisdom, after all, is the accumulation and application of knowledge(s), or differing cultural "truths;" that is, the ability to learn and grow.

Because queer-inclusive curricula work against heterosexism and homophobia to the advantage of all students, it would seem that teachers would be eager to engage with this kind of work. However, Blackburn has heard her students who are current and future teachers of ELA express reluctance to use LGBTQ material, just as Buckley has heard his younger college students bemoan the lack of such material when they were in high school. In Blackburn's Middle Childhood Literature course, she required her students, currently practicing teachers, to read [J.] Woodson's *From the Notebooks of Melanin Sun*. She chose it because the queer characters are adults rather than youths and because there are no sex scenes with same-sex couples. Of equal importance, she felt, was that the queer people in the book are racially diverse, which helped her to disabuse her students of the belief that only white people are gay. For all her efforts, however, she found that some of her students were offended simply because they were assigned to read the book and appalled by the suggestion that such a book is appropriate for middle school students. The most accepting members of her class expressed a willingness to share the book with individual students whom they knew to be struggling with queer-related issues. Yet even these voiced an unwillingness to share the book with their classes more generally because of their fear of creating controversy. . . .

How to Create a Queer-inclusive Classroom

Reading and writing are vehicles for thinking and feeling, and discussions, both small and large group, can facilitate thinking and feeling. Teachers must actively, honestly, and intellectually facilitate these discussions. Students, in other words, should have opportunities to play active roles in discussions, and teachers should listen intently to what their students have to say. In terms of queer-inclusive ELA curricula, discussions of same-sex desire need to be incorporated into larger discussions of diversity. Discussions of family, relationships, community, and discrimination can promote such incorporation. Literature should be contextualized with pertinent information that will guide students' understanding. Whether the texts are essays, novels, picture books, or films, teachers should carefully consider their students and communities, not to avoid differences of opinion but to include them in classroom discussions.

To that end, we want to suggest one possible approach to preparing a queer-inclusive ELA curriculum, one that offers students a variety of experiences with various and varying characters and narrators who define themselves by expressing desire for those identified as lesbian, gay, bisexual, transgender, or queer (who would suspend sexual and gender identities), or those who implicitly claim a "normal" identity. Our guiding pedagogical concern is how best to have students comprehend and critique the social binaries that have cultural currency in their own lives: for example young/old, logical/emotional, gay/straight. In other words, we want to provide students the opportunity to experience how we are all called into being. Yet we do not want to provide students a rigid script for what we hope will be their (re)experience of how they have identified.

We suggest that for secondary students, the teacher briefly describe a fictitious scenario of two couples who are members of the class. These students are more or less romantically involved. For example, Jill and Liz are attracted to each other, and Jill is also attracted to Seth, whose friends envy him for the apparent attention that the attractive Jill pays him. Jill's parents are supportive of what they term their daughter's "close relationship" with Liz. Neither Jill nor Liz is certain what this means, but they do know that Liz's parents (religious? conservative? uneducated?) are homophobic. The other couple is, let's say, Ron and Marlene, who have had sex, but want the romance of openly dating. Ron's father is African American and his mother is Asian American, and, although neither Marlene nor his friends seems to think anything of this, Marlene's mother often makes racist remarks.

After presenting the class with this brief scenario of make-believe students, we suggest forming small groups. Have each group complete a diary for each student for the week of an upcoming prom, adding an extra diary (but only one) if the group wants another person (student or adult) to be involved. Have the groups consider some or all of the following questions: "Who is supportive of whom?" "Who opposes whom?" "Why?" In other words, facilitate discussion by asking students to consider what any of us gains when we "act" as peers, parents, or religious leaders want. What do we gain by describing ourselves one way? What do we get by resisting one identity for the sake of another? How permanent is identity? Our goal is not merely to have students "try on" or consider the perspective of the "other." Rather, we hope that students come face to face with the personal and cultural contradictions that always follow the identity politics that make us part of a group or enable us to confront a group.

Although we believe it vital to interrupt familiar patterns of thinking and thereby "broaden possibilities for perceiving, interpreting, and representing experience," we also recognize that any curriculum needs to acknowledge its own entanglement in the "attitudes and biases, and issues of power related to language." "We need to be up front with our students in identifying our assumptions about literature," even those in which we two are very invested—the "queered curriculum" that assumes, as do we, that sexuality is a primary and "necessary companion to all knowing." To that end, we advocate a "queer-inclusive" ELA curricula designed and presented so that students, as maturing individuals, can "encompass opposed points of view," thus allowing them to "travel as far as possible away from *logos*, to explore how far *difference* can take us." As we see it, such an ELA curriculum is one way for all high school students to experience themselves amid "otherness," the "other" in their midst, and the contradictory "other" within us all.

The American Public Does Not Favor Gay Marriage

Paul R. Brewer and Clyde Wilcox

Paul R. Brewer is a professor in the Department of Journalism and Mass Communications at the University of Wisconsin— Milwaukee. Clyde Wilcox is a professor in the Department of Government at Georgetown University in Washington, D.C.

For many Americans, the issue of same-sex marriage burst upon the political scene in the fall of 2003, when the highest court in Massachusetts ruled that the state had no grounds to deny gay and lesbian couples the right to marry. Within a few months same-sex marriages were performed in a number of cities and counties, including large numbers of weddings in San Francisco, to widespread media attention. Religious conservatives pushed for a federal constitutional amendment that would ban same-sex marriage, which eventually won the backing of the president. Interest groups mobilized to "defend the equal rights" of same-sex couples to marry and to "defend the traditional family" by banning these marriages. Our purpose is to describe trends in public opinion about same-sex marriage, including public support for legal recognition for same-sex marriage, civil unions that would give same-sex couples some of the rights of legally married couples, and a proposed amendment to the U.S. constitution that would ban same-sex marriage.

Paul R. Brewer and Clyde Wilcox, "The Polls—Trends: Same-Sex Marriage and Civil Unions," *Public Opinion Quarterly*, vol. 69, no. 4, winter 2005, pp. 599–605, 607–615. Copyright © Paul R. Brewer and Clyde Wilcox 2005. Published by Oxford University Press on behalf of the American Association for Public Opinion Research. All rights reserved. Republished with permission, conveyed through Copyright Clearance Center, Inc., the authors and Oxford University Press.

Same-Sex Marriage Undermines Traditional Family

Viewed from a broader perspective, same-sex marriage is the latest front in a decades-old political struggle over gay rights. Other fronts in this contest have included the legal status of homosexual relations (as in the 1986 U.S. Supreme Court case *Bowers v. Hardwick*, which upheld the constitutionality of antisodomy laws, and the 2003 case *Lawrence v. Texas*, which overturned *Bowers*), employment nondiscrimination (the subject of a series of state initiatives in the late 1980s and 1990s, as well as the 1996 congressional vote on the Employment Non-Discrimination Act), and military service (as in the controversy over President Bill Clinton's 1993 push for "gays in the military"). The broad picture that has emerged from previous studies of public opinion about these issues is one of increasing public support for gay rights. Until recently, however, the existing polling data have provided little leverage on trends in public opinion about same-sex marriage. . . .

Drawing on the now-proliferating polling data, we offer a number of conclusions regarding public opinion about same-sex marriage. First, a majority of Americans consistently report seeing same-sex marriage as undermining the traditional American family or clashing with their own religious beliefs. Second, a substantial proportion of the public has followed the issue as of late, with the level of attention rising and falling in tandem with key events.

Third, a majority of citizens have opposed recognizing same-sex marriage from the earliest polls onward. One trend with two data points indicates a shift toward greater support from 1988 to 2004; from the early 1990s to the present, however, there is no sign of a dramatic trend toward greater support and some evidence of at least one ephemeral backlash. Fourth, the public has been more supportive of civil unions than of same-sex marriage, with support for such unions apparently increasing from 2000 to 2004 with at least one interruption. Support for civil unions is greater when respondents are primed to consider same-sex marriage in an earlier question in the interview. Fifth, the proportion of Americans who support at least some legal recognition of same-sex couples now exceeds the proportion of Americans who favor no recognition. Sixth, majorities have consistently supported inheritance rights, Social Security benefits, and health insurance benefits for gay spouses.

Seventh, a sizable proportion of the public has offered steady support for amending the constitution to define marriage as being between a man and a woman, but in most formulations this proportion constitutes either a slim majority or a roughly even split rather than a clear consensus. . . .

In 1988, 11 percent of respondents agreed that "homosexual couples should have the right to marry." . . . By 2004, the percentage agreeing had risen to 30 percent.

Two sets of polls indicate that stable majorities of Americans believe that same-sex marriage is incompatible with "family values" and their own religious beliefs. In a 1996 *Newsweek* poll, two-thirds of the respondents agreed that "gay marriage would go against [their] religious beliefs." Seven years later, the Pew Research Center for the People and the Press reported a 62 percent agreement rate. Likewise, both a 2000 Kaiser Family Foundation poll and a 2003 Pew poll found majorities in agreement with the statement that "allowing gays and lesbians to marry would undermine the traditional American family" . . .

Support for Same-Sex Marriage Increases Over Time

Though poll data about same-sex marriage are relatively sparse before 2003, two National Opinion Research Center surveys yield a trend that spans 16 years. In 1988, 11 percent of respondents agreed that "homosexual couples should have the right to marry," whereas 69 percent disagreed. By 2004, the percentage agreeing had risen to 30 percent, while the percentage disagreeing had declined to 54 percent.

Several organizations have collected trends on the topic dating as far back as the early to mid-1990s. Developments during this period included the 1993 Hawaii Supreme Court decision *Baehr v. Lewin*, which ruled that the state had shown no compelling interest in denying gays and lesbians equal rights to marriage, and the 1996 Defense of Marriage Act, which not only denied federal recognition of same-sex marriages but also allowed states to deny such recognition. Polls from the early to mid-1990s typically found that support for legal recognition for same-sex marriages was around or below 30 percent (e.g., 27 percent in a 1996 Gallup poll; 27 percent in a 1996 Pew poll; 27 percent, 27 percent, and 31 percent in 1992, 1993, and 1996 *Time*/CNN polls; 29 percent and 33 percent in 1994 and 1996 *Newsweek* polls).

The June 2003 decision in Lawrence v. Texas *may have inspired a backlash against gay rights.*

In contrast to public support for employment nondiscrimination protections and for military service by gays and lesbians, support for same-sex marriage rose modestly, if at all, from the early 1990s to the end of the decade or beyond. In polls from the late 1990s onward—which were much more numerous than polls in the early to mid-1990s—support ranged from the high 20s to the low 40s, depending on which organization asked the question, which question it asked, and when it asked the question. In no poll, however, did a majority support legal recognition. Indeed, the overall picture that emerges is one of striking stability.

To be sure, reports from a pair of polling organizations— Gallup and Pew—suggest that the June 2003 decision in

Lawrence v. Texas may have inspired a backlash against gay rights. Polls conducted by these organizations recorded drops in support four months following the decision: from 39 percent to 35 percent in Gallup and from 38 percent to 32 percent in Pew, although only the latter drop was clearly significant. Then again, this backlash, to the extent that it was genuine; seems to have been a temporary phenomenon. When one looks at the entire set of polls measuring public support for same-sex marriage, no durable trend in public support over the past few years emerges. Though Pew's measure has not returned to its pre-*Lawrence* high of 38 percent, Gallup's measure has (e.g., the 42 percent recorded in May 2004). Moreover, data from other polling organizations (*Time*/CNN, *Newsweek*, ABC News/*Washington Post*, *Investor's Business Daily*/*Christian Science Monitor*, Quinnipiac, NBC News/*Wall Street Journal*, and the National Annenberg Election Survey) suggest fairly constant levels of support in 2003 and 2004; the one exception is CBS News/*New York Times*, which found declining support from August 2003 (40 percent) to February 2004 (30 percent).

Gallup has conducted two polls measuring public support for same-sex marriage in 2005. One from March yielded the lowest level of support in the Gallup trend since 1996 (28 percent); another conducted a little more than a month later, however, placed support at 39 percent. Both figures came from relatively small samples.

Civil Unions Seen as a Compromise

Public support for civil unions—such as those recognized by Vermont in response to a 1999 decision by that state's Supreme Court—appears to be substantially greater than public support for same-sex marriage. This finding stands out most clearly in the nine (three Gallup, two ABC News/*Washington Post*, four Pew, and one Quinnipiac) polls that included questions about both same-sex marriage and civil unions: in these polls, the percentage supporting civil unions exceeded the percentage supporting same-sex marriage by at least 3 percentage points and by as much as 19 percentage points. The average difference was 14 percentage points.

It may be that civil unions are viewed as a compromise when respondents have first considered marriage.

The longest trend here—the one from Gallup that spans five years and includes eight data points—suggests shifts over time in support for civil unions. In the October 2000 Gallup poll, 42 percent favored civil unions and 54 percent opposed them. In May 2003 the percentages for support and opposition were both 49. Gallup then recorded a 9-point drop in support from May 2003 to July 2003 that was erased by a subsequent increase, another finding consistent with the notion of a temporary backlash against gay rights following *Lawrence v. Texas*.

Two polls that included experiments in question order, one from Pew (October 2003) and the other from Gallup (May 2004), suggest that support for civil unions may be shaped by the survey context. Pew found a higher level of support for civil unions (45 percent versus 37 percent) when the question was asked after a question about same-sex marriage than when the question was asked before a question about same-sex marriage. Gallup found a similar pattern (56 percent versus 49 percent). Thus, people appear to be more likely to express support for civil unions when they are first allowed to express opposition to same-sex marriage. It may be that civil unions are viewed as a compromise when respondents have first considered marriage. The Gallup survey experiment also indicated that support for same-sex marriage was lower when the civil unions question preceded the same-sex marriage question, but the Pew survey experiment did not produce a similar result.

Several polling organizations have collected trends for public opinion about a three-way choice between legal recognition of same-sex marriage, civil unions, or neither. These trend data are limited to 2004, with one exception: a 2000 Fox News/Opinion Dynamics poll showing that 47 percent of respondents favored no legal recognition, whereas 43 percent favored some recognition, whether in the form of marriage or "legal partnerships". In every poll conducted from 2004 onward, more respondents favored some sort of recognition than favored no recognition, with the difference exceeding the margin of error in every case except one (the February 2004 *Newsweek* poll;). In some of these polls (e.g., the *Newsweek* polls), those who favored some sort of recognition were divided fairly evenly between those who favored legal marriage and those who favored civil unions. The *Los Angeles Times* polls, on the other hand, found a substantial tilt toward civil unions rather than legal marriage. So did CBS News/*New York Times* polls from October 2004, November 2004, and February 2005. . . .

A Majority Supports Constitutional Ban

For public opinion about a constitutional amendment to define marriage as being between a man and woman, the longest trend line only goes back to July 2003—about the time that the post-*Lawrence* debate over such an amendment began. Opinion on the topic has varied little over the observed time span. Gallup, for example, has consistently found that around half or slightly more of the public supports "an amendment that would define marriage as being between a man and a woman, thus barring marriages between gay or lesbian couples," with opposition ranging from 37 percent to 47 percent. The *Time*/CNN, NBC News/*Wall Street Journal*, and *Los Angeles Times* trends are similar: in each, support for the amendment has had a slight advantage over or an approximately even split with opposition. Each organization used a question similar (but not identical) to the Gallup item, in that it mentioned defining marriage as being between a man and a woman, as well denying recognition to same-sex marriage.

Several exceptions to this pattern warrant mention. The University of Pennsylvania/National Annenberg Election Survey polls, which asked about "an amendment to the U.S. Constitution saying that no state can allow two men to marry each other or two women to marry each other," reported support at 40–43 percent and opposition at 48–50 percent, but even here the differences between support and opposition were within or nearly within the margin of error. These polls also yielded consistently high percentages of "don't know" responses (ranging from 8 percent to 11 percent). The ABC News/*Washington Post* trend is a more striking exception— particularly the January 2004 poll, which reported only 38 percent support for a constitutional amendment (with the other three polls in this trend putting support at 46 percent, 44 percent, and 44 percent). Note, however, that the question wording used here differed substantially from the wording used in other questions: it specified that the amendment would "make it illegal for homosexual couples to get married anywhere in the United States" and presented the alternative to the amendment as "each state mak[ing] its own laws on homosexual marriage."

The other exceptions are the two CBS News/*New York Times* trends. When respondents were asked whether they thought "that defining marriage as a union only between a man and a woman is important enough to be worth changing the Constitution for, or isn't it that kind of issue," sizable majorities preferred the latter option to the former (56 percent versus 38–40 percent). The second CBS News/ *New York Times* trend, in which support for the amendment outweighed opposition by margins ranging from 15 to 23 points, was almost a mirror image. Here, again, the question wording deviated from the typical pattern, this time by omitting any mention that the amendment would bar same-sex marriages. Interestingly, when the February 2004 CBS News poll asked a version of its question mentioning that the amendment would "outlaw marriages between people of the same sex," support was 51 percent (compared to 59 percent for the standard CBS News item asked in the same survey). This pattern of results fits with previous findings that survey respondents tend to be more willing to "not allow" a practice than to "forbid" (or in this case, "outlaw") it.

Taken as a whole, the polling data suggest that although a substantial proportion of the public has consistently favored a constitutional amendment to define marriage as being between a man and a woman, popular support does not approach the "supermajority" level often held to be the standard for successful amendment efforts. As noted by the Pew Research Center (2004), support on this proposed amendment is equivalent to or lower than several other "perennial" failed amendments, including ones on flag burning and school prayer.

The Vatican Must Get Tough on Gay Ordinations into the Priesthood

Rod Dreher

Rod Dreher is an editorial writer and columnist for The Dallas Morning News

The first thing to understand about the Catholic Church's pedophilia scandal is that it is not technically a pedophilia scandal. Despite the gruesome example of defrocked Boston priest John Geoghan, whose case started the current tidal wave of revelations, the overwhelming majority of priests who have molested minors are not pedophiles—that is, like Geoghan, among the rare adults sexually attracted to pre-pubescent children. They are, rather, "ephebophiles"—adults who are sexually attracted to post-pubescent youths, generally aged 12 to 17. And their victims have been almost exclusively boys.

Stephen Rubino, a New Jersey lawyer, says that of the over 300 alleged victims of priest sex abuse he has represented, roughly 85 percent are boys, and were teenagers when the abuse occurred. Dr. Richard Fitzgibbons, an eminent Catholic psychiatrist who has treated scores of victims and priest-perpetrators, says 90 percent of his patients were either teen male victims of priests, or priests who abused teen boys.

The Silent Scandals

"I think we have to ask the question: Why are 90 percent to 95 percent, and some estimates say as high as 98 percent, of the victims of clergy [abuse] teenage boys? . . . We need to ask that question, and I think there's a certain reluctance to raise that issue," said the Rev. Donald B. Cozzens, author of *The Changing Face of the Priesthood* on a recent *Meet the Press*.

This is chiefly a scandal about unchaste or criminal homosexuals in the Catholic priesthood.

The reluctance arises, no doubt, partly out of a fear of antagonizing homosexual anti-defamation groups, who resent the stereotype of male homosexuals as pederasts [men who have intimate relations with adolescents boys]. It's much safer to focus inquiry on the question of mandatory celibacy, or the issue of ordaining women. Yet it defies common sense to imagine that an ordinary man, having made a vow not to marry, is therefore going to be sexually attracted to boys. Indeed, suppose the Second Vatican Council in the 1960s had admitted married men to the ranks of the Catholic priesthood: Would a single adolescent boy molested over the past 40 years have escaped his fate? Similarly, if women had been ordained, would that somehow have made sexually predatory gay priests disappear?

No, this is chiefly a scandal about unchaste or criminal homosexuals in the Catholic priesthood, and about far too many in Church leadership disinclined to deal with the problem—or, worse, who may in some cases be actively involved in the misconduct. For Catholics, to start asking questions about homosexuality in the priesthood is to risk finding out more than many Church members prefer to know. For journalists, to confront the issue is to risk touching the electrified third rail of American popular culture: the dark side of homosexuality. Yet when we learn that the greatest crisis the Catholic Church in America has ever faced has been brought upon it almost wholly by male clerics seducing boys, attention must be paid to the man behind the curtain.

Gay Priests Are the Problem

It is true that a great many gay people are sickened and appalled by what these wicked priests have done to boys, and some with a public voice, like journalist Andrew Sullivan, have vigorously denounced it. At the same time, Sullivan has strongly supported the ministry of gay priests.

How many gay priests are there? No one can say with certainty; the American bishops have never formally studied the issue, and, for obvious reasons, it is all but impossible to determine an accurate number. Richard Sipe, a laicized priest and psychotherapist who has studied the phenomenon of priests and sex abuse for most of his 40-year career, believes 20 percent of Catholic priests are homosexual, and that half of those are sexually active. In his book, Fr. Cozzens cites various studies putting the total much higher, but these surveys typically suffer from methodological problems that skew the numbers upward.

The sexual abuse of minors is facilitated by a secret, powerful network of gay priests.

But those who lowball the numbers could equally be accused of wanting to downplay the problem. The Rev. C. John McCloskey, a member of the conservative Opus Dei organization, claimed recently that the number of gay priests is "two percent to four percent at a maximum," or equivalent to the estimated number of homosexuals in the general population; if that were true, however, it would be hard to explain why, according to experts, Catholic priests are dying of AIDS at a higher rate than males in the general population.

The raw numbers are less important, though, if homosexual priests occupy positions of influence in the vast Catholic bureaucracy; and there seems little doubt that this is the case in the American Church. Lest this be dismissed as right-wing paranoia, it bears noting that psychotherapist Sipe is no conservative—indeed, he is disliked by many on the Catholic Right for his vigorous dissent from Church teaching on sexual morality—yet he is convinced that the sexual abuse of minors is facilitated by a secret, powerful network of gay priests. Sipe has a great deal of clinical and research experience in this field; he has reviewed thousands of case histories of sexually active priests and abuse victims. He is convinced of the existence of what the Rev. Andrew Greeley, the left-wing clerical gadfly, has called a "lavender Mafia."

"This is a system. This is a whole community. You have many good people covering it up," Sipe says. "There is a network of power. A lot of seminary rectors and teachers are part of it, and they move to chancery-office positions, and on to bishoprics. It's part of the ladder of success. It breaks your heart to see the people who suffer because of this."

An especially nasty aspect of this phenomenon is the vulnerability of sexually active gay priests and bishops to manipulation via blackmail.

Militant Homosexuality in Seminaries

In his new book, *Goodbye! Good Men*, Michael S. Rose documents in shocking detail how pervasive militant homosexuality is in many seminaries, how much gay sex is taking place among seminarians and priest-professors, and how gay power cliques exclude and punish heterosexuals who oppose them. "It's not just a few guys in a few seminaries that have an ax to grind. It is a pattern," says Rose. "The protective network [of homosexual priests] begins in the seminaries."

The stories related in Rose's book will strike many as incredible, but they track closely with the stories that priests have told me about open gay sex and gay politicking in seminaries. The current scandal is opening Catholic eyes: As one ex-seminarian says, "People thought I was crazy when I told them what it was like there, so I finally quit talking about it. They're starting to see now that I wasn't."

Goodbye! Good Men links homosexuality among priests with theological dissent, a connection commonly made by conservative Catholics who wonder why their parish priests have practically abandoned teaching and explaining Catholic sexual morality. But one veteran vocations-team member for a conservative diocese cautions that Catholics should not assume that theological orthodoxy guarantees heterosexuality or chastity. "You find [active homosexuality] among some pretty conservative orders, and in places you'd not expect it," he says. "That's what makes this so depressing. You don't know where to turn."

An especially nasty aspect of this phenomenon is the vulnerability of sexually active gay priests and bishops to manipulation via blackmail. Priests, psychiatrists, and other informed parties say they encounter this constantly. "It's the secrecy," says Stephen Rubino. "If you're a bishop and you're having a relationship, and people know about it, are you compromised on dealing with sexually abusive priests? You bet you are. I've seen it happen."

Longtime observers predict that in the coming weeks, bishops and priests will be forced to resign under fire after their closeted homosexual lives, including sexual abuse, become public. The disgraced pederast former bishop of Palm Beach, Fla., is probably not alone. If this happens, the Vatican will face mounting pressure from the Catholic rank-and-file to take action. As Fr. Greeley has written, "The laity, I suspect, would say it is one thing to accept a homosexual priest and quite another to accept a substantially homosexual clergy, many of whom are blatantly part of the gay subculture."

The Vatican Opposes Gay Ordination

Rome has explicitly discouraged the ordination of homosexuals since at least 1961. For the past decade, the Vatican has been ratcheting up the pressure against gay ordination—to little avail in most U.S. dioceses. Last year, Archbishop Tarcisio Bertone, a top Vatican official, said gays should not be admitted to seminaries, a line that was reinforced in early March by the Pope's spokesman, Joaquin Navarro-Valls. Recent reports indicate that the Vatican may soon release another document to restate and clarify this policy.

We now have a culture in which there is little support for chastity, even from within the ranks of the Catholic priesthood.

Today, those who defend allowing homosexuals into the priesthood point to the Church's official teaching, which distinguishes between homosexual orientation (which the Church does not consider sinful) and homosexual acts (which the Catechism labels "grave depravity"). There is nothing wrong, the argument goes, with ordaining a homosexually oriented man committed to living chastely and to upholding the Church's teaching on sexuality. Surely there are many such faithful priests in service.

This argument, though, seems persuasive only under conditions far removed from those under which priests have to live today. We now have a culture in which there is little support for chastity, even from within the ranks of the Catholic priesthood. Conservative theologian Michael Novak says he is not prepared to argue for the exclusion of homosexuals from ordination, but as an ex-seminarian, he strongly believes gays should not be on seminary faculties, directing the formation in chastity of young men. Other Catholics who are more liberal than Novak on many Church issues go further on the question of gay ordination: Sipe believes gays shouldn't be admitted into seminaries at the present time—for their own protection, against sexual predators among the faculty and administration, who will attempt to draw them into a priestly subculture in which gay sex is normative behavior. Fr. Thomas P. Doyle, another critic of celibacy who has been deeply involved in the clergy-abuse issue, concurs: "Ordaining gay men at this time would be putting them, no matter how good and dedicated, in a precarious position."

Zero-Tolerance Policy

No one wants to stigmatize homosexuals as abusers, because most of them are not. Still, it's hard to gainsay the contention that if there were few homosexuals in the priesthood, the number of sex-abuse victims today would be drastically lower. "We're learning a significant lesson from all this," says Dr. Fitzgibbons. "We have to protect our young. The protection of children and teenagers is more important than the feelings of homosexuals."

Though the American scandal is nowhere near played out, it seems likely that the barrage of humiliating revelations and mounting financial losses will force the Vatican to get tough on gay ordinations. To have any hope of being effective, Rome will have to clean house at most American seminaries. This can be done only if local bishops can be trusted to be both loyal to Rome and resolute—and that will happen only if the Vatican forces them to be accountable.

The only sensible response, it would seem, is a zero-tolerance policy when it comes to sexual behavior by clergy.

That still leaves the problem of current and future priests who are both homosexual and unchaste. It is true that most of the abuse cases that have reached the public's attention today involve older priests, and the situation in the seminaries has apparently been reined in somewhat from the anything-goes heyday of the 1970s and 1980s. Nevertheless, the problem is still enormous. Most of the cases reported in *Goodbye! Good*

Men involving homosexual corruption date from recent years. One priest who left his seminary teaching post in the mid 1990s in despair over rampant homosexuality—and episcopal indifference to it—told me ominously: "The things I have seen in my years there are probably previews of coming attractions."

There is every reason to believe that a conservative reform ... would result in a tide of good men seeking holy orders.

The only sensible response, it would seem, is a zero-tolerance policy when it comes to sexual behavior by clergy, even between consenting adults (homosexual and heterosexual). The laity has a role to play as well. In a much-discussed essay in the November 2000 *Catholic World Report*, the Rev. Paul Shaughnessy, a Jesuit priest, suggested that lay Catholics seeking reform should help keep their priests accountable. He urged lay Catholics to use their checkbooks to fight sexual corruption, by steering their donations away from scandal-ridden dioceses and religious orders, and sending them instead to clean groups like Mother Teresa's Missionaries of Charity—and then letting the bishop or religious order know what they've done and why.

Conservative Reform Is Needed

There is tremendous fear among churchmen that the kind of changes needed to put the Church aright will result in a severe loss of numbers in the priesthood at a time when vocations are already at a historic low. That is probably true in the short run, but the experience of a handful of American dioceses in which the local bishop is openly orthodox and willing to defend Church teaching without compromise gives reason to hope that a strong dose of traditional medicine can go a long way toward curing the Church's ills.

In 1995, Archbishop Elden Curtiss of Omaha published an article pointing out that dioceses that promote rigorous fidelity to Church teaching and practice produce significantly more vocations than do the moderate to liberal majority. Seminaries like Mount Saint Mary's in Emmitsburg, Md.—where men know they will be supported in their authentic Catholic beliefs and practices, and in their commitment to celibacy and chastity—are filled to capacity.

This is not to suggest that the crisis now gripping the Catholic Church in America can be entirely solved by a restoration of rigorously orthodox theology. Another problem that has to be addressed is the clericalist bias seriously afflicting the judgment of many bishops: Even Curtiss himself erred recently, by keeping an Omaha priest in ministry after the priest admitted having a child-pornography problem. But a return to the basics has to be a big part of a comprehensive solution. There is every reason to believe that a conservative reform—replacing dissenting or milquetoast bishops with solid, no-nonsense men; making the seminaries safe places for heterosexuals loyal to Church teaching; and restoring the priesthood to a corps of chaste, faith-filled disciples—would result in a tide of good men seeking holy orders.

This has already been happening in dioceses like Omaha; Lincoln, Neb.; Denver; Peoria, Ill.; Fargo, N.D.; and Arlington, Va. The road map that points the way to an authentic renewal of the Catholic priesthood is being drawn up in those places. And if you want to see the alternative—what would happen if the U.S. Church simply stayed on its current course—just read the morning papers.

Public School Children Should Not Be Indoctrinated with Queer Theory

Marjorie King

Marjorie King is a freelance writer.

At a high school in prosperous Newton, Massachusetts, it's "To B GLAD Day"—or, less delicately, Transgender, Bisexual, Gay, Lesbian Awareness Day. An advocacy session for students and teachers features three self-styled transgendered individuals—a member of the senior class and two recent graduates. One of the transgenders, born female, announces that "he" had been taking hormones for 16 months. "Right now I am a 14-year-old boy going through puberty and a 55-year-old woman going through menopause," she complains. "I am probably the moodiest person in the world." A second panelist declares herself an "androgyne in between both genders of society." She adds, "Gender is just a bunch of stereotypes from society, but I am completely personal, and my gender is fluid."

Only in liberal Massachusetts could a public school endorse such an event for teens, you might think. But you would be wrong. For the last decade or so, largely working beneath public or parental notice, a well-organized movement has sought to revolutionize the curricula and culture of the nation's public schools. Its aim: to stamp out "hegemonic heterosexuality"—the traditional view that heterosexuality is the norm—in favor of a new ethos that does not just tolerate homosexuality but instead actively endorses experimenting with it, as well as with a polymorphous range of bisexuality, transgenderism, and transsexuality. The educational establishment, has enthusiastically signed on. What this portends for the future of the public schools and the psychic health of the nation's children is deeply worrisome.

Origins of Queer Theory

This movement to "queer" the public schools, as activists put it, originated with a shift in the elite understanding of homosexuality. During the eighties, when gay activism first became a major cultural force, homosexual leaders launched a campaign that mirrored the civil rights movement. To claim their rights, homosexuals argued (without scientific evidence) that their orientation was a genetic inheritance, like race, and thus deserved the same kind of civil protections the nation had guaranteed to blacks. An inborn, unchangeable fact, after all, could not be subject to moral disapproval. There ensued a successful effort to normalize homosexuality throughout the culture, including a strong push for homosexual marriage, gays in the military, and other signs of civic equality.

For the queer theorist, all unambiguous and permanent notions of a natural sexual or gender identity are coercive impositions on our individual autonomy.

But even as the homosexual-rights campaign won elite endorsement and lavish funding, even as supportive organizations proliferated, the gay movement began to split internally. By the early nineties, many gay activists viewed goals such as gay marriage or domestic partner unions as lamely "assimilationist"—an endorsement of standards of behavior that "queers," as they called themselves, should reject as oppressively "straight." And they militantly began defending the "queer lifestyle" not as an ineluctable fate but as the result of a fully conscious choice.

Underlying this militant stance was a radical new academic ideology called "queer theory." A mixture of the neo-

Freudianism of counterculture gurus Norman O. Brown and Herbert Marcuse and French deconstruction, queer theory takes to its extreme limit the idea that all sexual difference and behavior is a product of social conditioning, not nature. It is, in their jargon, "socially constructed." For the queer theorist, all unambiguous and permanent notions of a natural sexual or gender identity are coercive impositions on our individual autonomy—our freedom to reinvent our sexual selves whenever we like. Sexuality is androgynous, fluid, polymorphous—and therefore a laudably subversive and even revolutionary force.

Rutgers English professor Michael Warner, a leading queer theorist, observes that categories like "heterosexual" and "homosexual" are part of "the regime of the normal" that queer theory wants to explode. "What identity," he writes, "encompasses queer girls who f*&k queer boys with strap-ons, or FTMs (female-to-male transsexuals) who think of themselves as queer, FTMs who think of themselves as straights, or FTMs for whom life is a project of transition and screw the categories anyway?" To overturn the old dichotomies of hetero/homo and even male/female, Warner encourages continuous sexual experimentation.

[GLSEN] seeks to transform the culture and instruction of every public school, so that children will learn to equate "heterosexism" . . . with other evils like racism and sexism.

A relatively recent arrival on college campuses, queer theory has swiftly dominated the myriad university gender-studies programs and spread its influence to other disciplines, too, "queering" everything under the sun. Type "queering" into Amazon.com's search engine, and up comes *Queering the Middle Ages, Queering the Color Line, Queering India*, and many other books, many from prestigious academic presses.

The Queering of Schools

It would be tempting to dismiss queer theory as just another intellectual fad, with little influence beyond the campus, if not for gay activists' aggressive effort to introduce the theory's radical view of sexuality into the public schools. Leading the effort is the Gay, Lesbian and Straight Educational Network (GLSEN, pronounced "glisten"), an advocacy group founded a decade ago to promote homosexual issues in the public schools. It now boasts 85 chapters, four regional offices, and some 1,700 student clubs, called "gay/straight alliances," that it has helped form in schools across the country.

A 2002 GLSEN conference in Boston held a seminar . . . that examined ways of setting 'the tone for nontraditional gender role play' for preschoolers.

GLSEN often presents itself as a civil rights organization, saying that it is only after "tolerance" and "understanding" for a victim group. Sometimes, therefore, it still speaks the old gay-rights language of unchangeable homosexual "identity" and "orientation." But it is, in fact, a radical organization that has clearly embraced the queer-theory worldview. It seeks to transform the culture and instruction of every public school, so that children will learn to equate "heterosexism"—the favoring of heterosexuality as normal—with other evils like racism and sexism and will grow up pondering their sexual orientation and the fluidity of their sexual identity.

That GLSEN embraces queer theory is clear from the addition of transgendered students to the gays and lesbians the group claims to represent. By definition, the transgendered are those who choose to change their gender identity by demeanor, dress, hormones, or surgery. Nothing could be more profoundly opposed to the notion of a natural sexual identity. Consider as evidence of queer theory's influence, too, the GLSEN teachers' manual that says that middle-schoolers "should have the freedom to explore [their] sexual orientation and find [their] own unique expression of lesbian, bisexual, gay, straight, or any combination of these." What is this but Michael Warner's appeal to pansexual experimentation?

One of the major goals of GLSEN and similar groups is to reform public school curricula and teaching so that Lesbian, Gay, Bisexual, Transgender—or LGBT—themes are always central and always presented in the approved light. GLSEN holds regular conferences for educators and activists with workshops bearing titles such as "Girls Will Be Boys and Boys Will Be Girls: Creating a Safe, Supportive School Environment for Trans, Intersex, Gender Variant and Gender Questioning Youth" and "Developing and Implementing a Transgender In-clusive Curriculum." Every course in every public school should focus on LGBT issues, GLSEN believes. A workshop at GLSEN's annual conference in Chicago in 2000 complained that "most LGBT curricula are in English, history and health" and sought ways of introducing its agenda into math and sci-ence classes, as well. (As an example of how to queer geom-etry, GLSEN recommends using gay symbols such as the pink triangle to study shapes.)

Queer Theory Educational Products

Nor is it ever too early to begin stamping out heterosexism. A 2002 GLSEN conference in Boston held a seminar on "Gender in the Early Childhood Classroom" that examined ways of set-ting "the tone for nontraditional gender role play" for *pre-schoolers*. To help get the LGBT message across to younger children, teachers can turn to an array of educational prod-ucts, many of them available from GLSEN. Early readers in-clude *One Dad, Two Dads, Brown Dad, Blue Dads; King and King*; and *Asha's Mums*.

As for teaching aids, a 1999 book, *Queering Elementary Education*, with a foreword by GLSEN executive director Kevin Jennings, offers essays on "Locating a Place for Gay and Lesbian Themes in Elementary Reading, Writing and Talking" and "How to Make 'Boys' and 'Girls' in the Classroom"—the scare quotes showing the queer theorist's ever present belief that categorizing gender is a political act.

For comprehensiveness, nothing beats a GLSEN-recommended resource manual distributed to all K-12 public schools in Saint Paul and Minneapolis. The manual presents an educational universe that filters everything through an LGBT lens. Lesson ideas include "role playing" exercises to "counter harassment," where students pretend, say, to be bisexual and hear hurtful words cast at them; testing students to see where their attitudes lie toward sexual "difference" (mere tolerance is unacceptable; much better is "admiration" and, best of all, "nurturance"); getting students to take a "Sexual Orientation Quiz"; and having heterosexual students learn 37 ways that heterosexuals are privileged in society. In turn, principals should make an "ongoing PA announcement"—once a week, the manual says—telling students about confidential support programs for LGBT students.

No organization has been more steadfast in its support of GLSEN than the NEA.

Teachers, the manual suggests, should demand that public school students memorize the approved meanings of important LGBT words and terms, from "bigenderist" to "exotophobia." Sometimes, these approved meanings require Orwellian redefinitions: "Family: Two or more persons who share resources, share responsibility for decisions, share values and goals, and have commitments to one another over a period of time . . . regardless of blood, or adoption, or marriage." . . .

Teachers' Unions Support Queer Indoctrination

Though many parents aren't aware of it yet, the agenda has moved far beyond the wishful thinking of activists. The keynote speaker at GLSEN's 2000 conference was Robert Chase, president of the 2.7 million-member National Education Association, the nation's biggest, most powerful teachers' union. The program booklet for the event featured greetings not only from Chase but from then-president Clinton, Chicago mayor Richard Daley, and the head of the American Federation of Teachers, the second-biggest U.S. teachers' union. The celebratory notes expressed the kind of praise once reserved for groups like the Boy Scouts. A long list of well-known organizations has backed LGBT programs in the classroom, including the American Psychiatric Association, the American Library Association, and the National Association of Social Workers.

No organization has been more steadfast in its support of GLSEN than the NEA. During the NEA's annual convention in July 2001, many observers expected the teachers' union to pass an official resolution incorporating GLSEN's sweeping educational goals into K-12 curricula nationwide. As it turns out, the NEA, clearly trying to minimize public awareness of an unprecedented infringement on parental prerogatives, tabled the resolution and announced a task force to study how best to approach LGBT issues in the schools. But in February 2002, the NEA board of directors approved the task force's report—a pure emanation of the GLSEN worldview, as is clear both from its numerous citations of GLSEN documents in the footnotes and from its recommendations.

Following the task force's lead, the NEA will now struggle to expunge "heterosexism" from the consciousness of children in the classroom. The union has encouraged schools to integrate LGBT themes into curricula, instructional material, and programs; to emphasize the legitimacy of different "family structures," including domestic partner arrangements; and to offer counseling services for students struggling with their "sexual/gender orientation." Small wonder that GLSEN greeted the NEA task force's report, and its endorsement by the union, with hosannas. "These powerful new recommendations signal that help is on the way for lesbian, gay, bisexual and transgender students and staff who experience day-to-day abuse in America's schools," enthused GLSEN head Jennings.

Queering Education Takes Root Nationally

The queering of the public schools has perhaps advanced furthest in California, where a new state law requires public schools to teach all K-12 students (and K means *five-year-olds*) "to appreciate various sexual orientations." What the new law might mean in practice, warned a state assemblyman, was on display at Santa Rosa High School, where invited homosexual activists "talked about using cellophane during group sex and said that 'clear is best because you can see what you want to lick,'" or at Hale Middle School in Los Angeles, where during an AIDS education course, "12-year-olds were subjected to graphic descriptions of anal sex and tips on how to dispose of used condoms so parents don't find out." As the assemblyman noted, sex ed courses throughout California public schools, influenced heavily by national sex education advocates SEICUS and Planned Parenthood, have already enthusiastically endorsed the GLSEN worldview.

School districts that refuse to go along with the homosexual agenda now must contend with the American Civil Liberties Union.

But California is only the cutting edge: efforts to queer the schools are under way in many other locales, from Massachusetts to Oregon. The co-chair of the Massachusetts Governor's Commission on Gay and Lesbian Youth, for example, informs the *Boston Globe* that teachers across that state are increasingly integrating LGBT themes into lessons—discussing the sexual orientation of authors as an interpretive tool in literature classes, she says, or comparing gay and bisexual with straight student mental health data in order to study percentages. After a ferocious battle, the Broward School Board in Florida recently voted to rely on GLSEN to train teachers in LGBT "sensitivity." In Gresham, Oregon, in early 2002, school officials at Centennial High School brought in gay and lesbian speakers in English, drama, and health classes during the school's annual "diversity" week, neither telling students about it beforehand nor letting them opt out of the classes if they wanted. Parental anger forced school officials to issue a public apology. . . .

Dissenting Schools Face Lawsuits

Parents or other concerned citizens who complain about any aspect of the queering of public education can face withering attacks, not just from gay activists but from cultural elites in general. When the two members of the Parents' Rights Coalition released their tape of the GLSEN-sponsored fisting workshop to the public, to take one typical example, the *Boston Globe* didn't condemn the use of public funds and state employees to instruct schoolchildren in an arcane and dangerous "sexual" practice; instead, it denounced the whistleblowers as fomenters of "intolerance."

School districts that refuse to go along with the homosexual agenda now must contend with the American Civil Liberties Union, too. The ACLU's Lesbian and Gay Rights Project has launched a national effort, called "Every Student, Every School," that plans to sue on First Amendment grounds any school that refuses gay/straight student clubs on its premises. Already, schools in Kentucky and Texas face legal action.

No compulsory public school system can be justified unless what it teaches is a worldview that the taxpayers who fund it can support. The "common schools" came into existence, after all, to acculturate immigrants to American values. For schools to try to indoctrinate children in a radical, minority worldview like that promoted by GLSEN and its allies—a vision that will form those children's values and shape their sense of selfhood—is a kind of tyranny, one that, in addition, intentionally drives a wedge between parents and children and, as queer theorist Michael Warner boasts, "opposes society itself." We must not let an appeal to our belief in tolerance and decency blind us to indecency—and to the individual and social damage that will result from it.

CHAPTER 4

Should Government Sanction Gay and Lesbian Relationships?

Chapter Preface

In November 2003, the Massachusetts Supreme Court, in *Goodridge v. Massachusetts Department of Public Health*, (40 Mass. 309) unwittingly played a major role in numerous 2004 elections when it ruled that civil marriage solely between a man and a woman was unconstitutional. The 4–3 decision overturned centuries of state jurisprudence. In 1692, when Plymouth and Massachusetts Bay colonies, Martha's Vineyard, Nantucket, Maine, and parts of Nova Scotia were merged into the colony of Massachusetts, the General Court enacted new laws, including the common law definition of marriage. Since that time, the Massachusetts Supreme Court contended, the state had violated the individual liberty and equal protection rights of homosexuals by not amending the marriage laws to include same-sex couples. The marriage statute, according to the court, "is rooted in persistent prejudices against persons who are (or who are believed to be) homosexual." Instead of interpreting marriage as a union between one man and one woman, the court, in its landmark ruling, construes it to mean "the voluntary union of two persons as spouses, to the exclusion of others."

The crux of this debate is whether or not homosexuality is an immutable characteristic or, to put it another way, if people become homosexuals because of nature or nurture. The Massachusetts court, similar to a 1993 Hawaii Supreme Court same-sex marriage decision (*Baehr v. Lewin* 74 Haw. 530), took the position that one's sex—and by extension one's sexual orientation—is biologically fated or natural and thereby entirely impervious to environmental influence. Based on this premise, the Bay State court held that it was "irrational" on the part of the legislature to argue that confining marriage to opposite-sex couples ensures that children are raised in the "optimal" setting. In fact, the court opined that because Massachusetts did not endorse gay and lesbian parenthood as the equivalent of being raised by one's married biological parents, the legislature unnecessarily penalized children by depriving their same-sex parents of the benefits, protections, and rights that flow from marriage. The court gave the legislature 180 days to "take such action as it may deem appropriate in light of this opinion." More than 8,500 same sex couples have married in Massachusetts since it became legal in May 2004.

According to gay marriage critics, sexual orientation, unlike the immutable characteristics of race and gender, is to a large extent behavioral. As a result, gays and lesbians have no constitutional right to marry. From their perspective, the Massachusetts court decision has nationwide implications because by legalizing gay marriages it may force individual states, through the Full Faith and Credit Clause of the federal constitution, to recognize the laws and judicial findings authorizing same-sex marriages. The decision is also important because to its detractors it is another example of "judicial activism," whereby state courts are ordering legislatures to permit same-sex marriages or a statutory equivalent alternative. In 1996, a Hawaiian court, in *Baehr v. Miiike* (91-1394) ruled that the Department of Health failed to show a compelling interest to deny gays and lesbians the right to marry. In 1998, an Alaskan court, in *Brause and Dugan v. Alaska* (3AN-95-6562), opined that the Bureau of Vital Statistics violated homosexuals' equal protection rights because "the decision to choose one's life partner is fundamental and that such a choice may include persons of the same sex." Likewise, a year later, the Vermont Supreme Court, in *Baker v. Vermont* (98-032) while not overturning state marriage statutes, ordered the legislature to enact legislation providing an equivalent statutory alternative for same-sex couples. In the cases of Hawaii and Alaska, state voters responded to these judicial decisions by amending their constitutions to preserve marriage for opposite-sex couples. It is important to note that the Massachusetts Supreme Court decision differs from the Vermont Supreme Court in an important way. Whereas the latter court recognizes civil unions, the Massachusetts Supreme Court, in an advisory opinion to the Senate, ruled that a civil union alternative would be unconstitutional. Gays and lesbians must be allowed to marry even though a proposed civil union bill would extend to homosexual couples the exact same protections and benefits as traditional marriages.

The 2003 Massachusetts Supreme Court decision is widely seen as playing a major role in many elections in 2004. Fearing that the court decision may force individual states to recognize same-sex marriages, thirteen states passed ballot initiatives on whether their state constitutions should include a ban on gay marriage. More than twenty million voted on the measures, which triumphed overall by a 2-to-1 ratio. In the four Southern states, the amendments received at least three-quarters of the votes, including 86 percent in Mississippi; the closest outcome was in Oregon, where the ban got 56 percent. More importantly, states with gay marriage ballot measures, particularly in the key state of Ohio, mobilized socially conservative Catholics and Protestants to support President George W. Bush and helped him to defeat Democratic candidate John Kerry.

Same-Sex Marriage Opponents Use Fear to Block Equality Under the Law

Evan Wolfson

Evan Wolfson is the executive director of Freedom to Marry, the gay and non-gay partnership working to win marriage equality nationwide.

The justices of the Massachusetts Supreme Judicial Court had hardly hung up their robes after issuing their landmark marriage-equality decision in November 2003 when that state's governor, Mitt Romney, declared his biggest quarrel with the majority opinion: The history-making ruling, he said, itself flies in the face of history.

Instead of complying with the constitutional command of equality, Governor Romney said he would lead the charge to amend the Massachusetts state constitution, one of the first constitutions in the world (older than even the United States), written by John Adams himself. The amendment to block marriage equality, the governor told ABC's *Good Morning America*, will "conform [to] three thousand years of human history, saying that marriage is between a man and a woman."

I'm sure many history buffs across the country choked on their morning coffee when they heard this assertion. I was a little surprised, in fact, that *Good Morning America* host Charles Gibson didn't do the same. Three *thousand* years of human history? While I have no doubt that Governor Romney is a well-educated man—he earned degrees from both Harvard and Brigham Young, after all—he seems to have forgotten some important parts of the history of marriage, including its recent history right here in America in our lifetimes.

Marriage Has Changed over Time

But since many of the opponents of marriage equality like to make this claim—"marriage has always been between a man and a woman for three, five, six thousand years," depending on the day, "and it shouldn't change"—here are a few years and a few changes in the past millennia of marriage that they are leaving out of the picture, borrowed in part from E. J. Graff's illuminating tour through the history of marriage, *What Is Marriage For? The Strange Social History of Our Most Intimate Institution*:

- 950 B.C.: King Solomon follows the tradition of the day, which dictates that lesser kings give a daughter's hand in marriage in order to seal a treaty with a more powerful king, and finds himself with seven hundred wives and three hundred concubines.

- 1400 A.D.: Parents in France and Holland have the legal authority to veto a daughter's choice of spouse until she turns twenty-five and a son's choice until he turns thirty.

- 1775: Married women lose the right to own property, make contracts, or file lawsuits after Lord Blackstone, widely considered an architect of British common law, declares that "husband and wife are one person, and the husband is that person."

- 1863: Alabama passes a law forbidding marriage between members of different races, later enshrined in the state constitution and only removed in the year 2000 (with 40 percent of voters still voting to keep it in).

- 1907: Governor Romney's father is born in Chihuahua, Mexico, where Mormon settlers moved, in part to avoid harassment under U.S. laws forbidding polygamy.

Were Romney serious on *Good Morning America*, the history he presumably would be seeking to defend would entitle him to marry the (white) first daughters of the less populated states of Rhode Island, Maine, New Hampshire, and Vermont—submerging their property and legal personhood into his. Such is the history of marriage that the governor claims to "defend."

Gay Marriage Is Not a Threat

Or maybe that's not what he had in mind.

The opponents of marriage equality . . . are . . . channeling Chicken Little in order to scare Americans away from supporting full marriage equality as the Constitution requires.

Perhaps Romney and other opponents have forgotten all the many changes that have taken place in the institution of marriage throughout history and in recent decades, changes that have taken marriage from being a dynastic or property arrangement to what we think of it as today: a committed union between equals based on love, commitment, self-sacrifice, hope, sharing, companionship, consent, and responsibility for the person of your choice.

Or, more likely, the opponents of marriage equality haven't really forgotten about these changes and battles and are instead, for political purposes, channeling Chicken Little in order to scare Americans away from supporting full marriage equality as the Constitution requires. Just what *will* happen now that Massachusetts, like most of Canada, has ended gay couples' exclusion from marriage? Or when California and

Connecticut or New Jersey and Oregon follow suit? Will our neighbors' marriages fail? Will same-sex couples use up all the marriage licenses? Will heterosexuals quit the marriage "club"? Will, as Chicken Little suggested so many times, the sky fall?

As more and more Americans, including more and more judges and journalists, begin asking the question "Just how would it harm someone to allow others to marry?" opponents of gay couples' right to marry have yet to explain exactly what the consequences of ending marriage discrimination against gay people would be, even as they push to plaster discrimination into our federal and state constitutions. Maybe smarter politicians such as Romney don't attempt that extra step of actually explaining because they learned a thing or two from the experience of U.S. Senator Rick Santorum, Republican of Pennsylvania, who took a stab at fleshing out the answer and laid bare the hollowness of the opposition's case.

"If the Supreme Court says that you have the right to consensual sex within your home," Santorum told an Associated Press reporter in April 2003, explaining why he believed the U.S. Supreme Court should not overturn the discriminatory Texas law against private consensual sex for gay Americans,

> then you have the right to bigamy, you have the right to polygamy, you have the right to incest, you have the right to adultery. You have the right to anything. All of those things are antithetical to a healthy, stable, traditional family. And that's sort of where we are in today's world, unfortunately. It all comes from, I would argue, this right to privacy that doesn't exist, in my opinion, in the United States Constitution.

Moving on from his rejection not just of gay people's right to have sex in their own home, but also of the Supreme Court's 1965 right-to-privacy decision in a case involving the right of married heterosexuals to use contraception without government interference, the senator almost offhandedly added, "That's not to pick on homosexuality. It's not, you know, man on child, man on dog, or whatever the case may be."

Most Americans understand that respecting equality under the law and saying that the government can't dictate the life choices of gay or non-gay couples is what conservatives used to stand for.

Senator Santorum's comments were almost immediately understood as extremist by the many Americans—gay and non-gay alike—who believe that the Supreme Court was right to say as long ago as 1965 that choices about whether or not to use contraceptives, or have a family, or have sex, properly belong to individuals, not the government. The AP reporter who was interviewing Santorum at the time admitted to astonishment at the senator's explanation. "I'm sorry, I didn't think I was going to talk about 'man on dog sex' with a United States senator—it's sort of freaking me out," she told Santorum.

Most Americans understand that respecting equality under the law and saying that the government can't dictate the life choices of gay or non-gay couples is what conservatives used to stand for, an affirmation of our American idea of freedom and limited government, not a rush to the "right to anything."

Gay Marriage Is a Civil Right

But just how different was the senator's attack on the U.S. Supreme Court from the governor's comments following the Massachusetts marriage ruling? True, Romney didn't repeat Santorum's candid admission that he is not just against gay equality in marriage, but also against choice in contraception and against the right to privacy, too. Ending the denial of marriage rights to gay people won't contradict human history, lead to polygamy or "man on dog" sex, or be a threat to kids, just as it won't lead to the sky falling. And I'd be willing to bet that Governor Romney and Senator Santorum know this just as well as you and I do. They must also know that the only way they are adhering to history in their extraordinary efforts to block the civil rights of gay people is in the "sky is falling" arguments they're employing. These scare tactics are anything but new. Romney and Santorum, like most of the opponents of marriage equality today, are echoing familiar claims from the many past struggles that have taken place (and are still taking place) on the battlefield of marriage rights in America.

Consider, for example, these other examples of gloom and doom compiled in a 1996 column by the *Chicago Tribune's* Eric Zorn:

1. A Republican senator from Wisconsin says marriages between gay couples must be forbidden "simply because natural instinct revolts at it as wrong."

2. An anti-gay group declares that extending the right to marry to gay couples would result in "a degraded and ignoble population incapable of moral and intellectual development." Group members say they based their stand on the "natural superiority with which God [has] ennobled heterosexuals."

3. A psychologist says "the tendency to classify all persons who oppose gay marriage as 'prejudiced' is in itself prejudice." He added, "Nothing of any significance is gained by such a marriage."

4. A Georgia lawmaker states that allowing gay people to marry "necessarily involves [the] degradation" of conventional marriage, an institution that "deserves admiration rather than execration."

5. A Kentucky congressman warns, "The next step will be that gays and lesbians will demand a law allowing them, without restraint, to . . . have free and unrestrained social intercourse with your unmarried sons and daugh-

ters." He adds: "It is bound to come to that. There is no disguising the fact. And the sooner the alarm is given and the people take heed, the better it will be for our civilization."

6. A Missouri judge rules, "When people of the same sex marry, they cannot possibly have any progeny . . . And such a fact sufficiently justifies those laws which forbid their marriage."

7. A Virginia state law says marriages between gay couples are "abominable" and would "pollute" American society.

8. In denying the appeal of a same-sex couple that tried to marry, a Georgia court rules that such marriages are "not only unnatural, but—always productive of deplorable results," such as increased effeminate behavior in the population. "They are productive of evil, and evil only, without any corresponding good . . . [in accordance with] the God of nature."

9. A congressman from Illinois opines that bans against the freedom to marry are not unconstitutional because they apply "equally to men and women."

10. Attorneys for the state of Tennessee say gay and lesbian couples should be prevented from marrying because they are "distasteful to our people and unfit to produce the human race. . . ." The state supreme court agrees, ruling that extending the freedom to marry would be "a calamity full of the saddest and gloomiest portent to the generations that are to come after us."

11. Lawyers for the state of California say a law preventing gay people from marrying is necessary to prevent "traditional marriage from being contaminated by the recognition of relationships that are physically and mentally inferior [and entered into by] the dregs of society."

12. In response to a lawsuit challenging Virginia's anti-gay-marriage law, a state judge rules, "The law concerning marriages is to be construed and understood in relation to those persons only to whom that law relates ... and not to a class of person clearly not within the idea of the legislature when contemplating the subject of marriage."

If there is one solid lesson about marriage that we can take by examining three thousand years of human history ... it is that the sky doesn't fall ... when people are able to choose whether and whom to marry.

The kicker in Zorn's column is that these twelve statements were not, in fact, made about gay people's freedom to marry. They actually were made between 1823 and 1964 by opponents of interracial marriage and African-Americans' equal citizenship. Zorn replaced the references to race with references to sexual orientation to underscore how today's battle over gay people's freedom to marry is not just about gay and lesbian people. It is a chapter in a civil rights struggle as old as the institution of marriage itself, a struggle that has also been borne by women seeking equality, people seeking to marry others of a different race, adults seeking to make their own decisions about parenting and sex, and married couples seeking an end to failed or abusive unions.

Gay Marriages Work in Canada

Look again at the twelve statements Eric Zorn quoted and switch them back, replacing the references to sexual orientation with references to race. How absurd it seems today to suggest that interracial couples can't procreate, that they are mentally and physically inferior, or that they cause the contamination of young children's minds. Read as arguments to justify continuing race discrimination in marriage, accepted not so long ago as part of the "definition" of marriage and God's own plan, it is easy to see them today as laughable (until we remember that real people were blocked for centuries in their desire to marry the person of their choice by the laws that opponents of equality fiercely defended).

Now take the exercise a step further. Imagine how preposterous similar statements regarding the need to "defend" marriage against committed gay couples will sound thirty years from now.

If there is one solid lesson about marriage that we can take by examining three thousand years of human history—or by looking across the border to Canada—it is that the sky doesn't fall, even if Niagara Falls still does, when people are able to choose whether and whom to marry, and are accorded equal treatment under the law.

The history of marriage is a history of change. In fact, in our lifetimes, right here in America, there have been at least four major changes in the legal institution of marriage. Each of them was at least as "sweeping," at least as big a departure from the conception and traditions of the day, and at least as hotly contested as is the proposal today to end sex discrimination in marriage.

Allowing Gay Marriage Is Not Like Sanctioning Polygamy

William Saletan

William Saletan is a national correspondent for Slate, *a daily online publication.*

Uh oh. Conservatives are starting to hyperventilate again. You know the symptoms: In a haystack of right-wing dominance, they find a needle of radicalism, declare it a mortal danger to civilization, and use it to rally their voters in the next election. First it was flag-burning. Then it was the "war on Christmas." Now it's polygamy. Having crushed gay marriage nationwide in 2004, they need to gin up a new threat to the family. They've found it in *Big Love*, the HBO series about a guy with three wives. Open the door to gay marriage, they warn, and group marriage will be next.

My friend Charles Krauthammer makes the argument succinctly in the *Washington Post*. "Traditional marriage is defined as the union of (1) two people of (2) opposite gender," he observes. "If, as advocates of gay marriage insist, the gender requirement is nothing but prejudice, exclusion and an arbitrary denial of one's autonomous choices," then "on what grounds do they insist upon the traditional, arbitrary and exclusionary number of two?"

Jealousy Undermines Polygamy

Here's the answer. The number isn't two. It's one. You commit to one person, and that person commits wholly to you. Second, the number isn't arbitrary. It's based on human nature. Specifically, on jealousy.

In an excellent *Weekly Standard* article against gay marriage and polygamy, Stanley Kurtz of the Hudson Institute discusses several recent polygamous unions. In one case, "two wives agreed to allow their husbands to establish a public and steady sexual relationship." Unfortunately, "one of the wives remains uncomfortable with this arrangement," so "the story ends with at least the prospect of one marriage breaking up." In another case, "two bisexual-leaning men meet a woman and create a threesome that produces two children, one by each man." Same result: "the trio's eventual breakup."

Fidelity isn't natural, but jealousy is.

Look up other articles on polygamy, even sympathetic ones, and you'll see the pattern. A Columbia News Service report on last month's national conference of polyamorists— people who love, but don't necessarily marry, multiple partners—features Robyn Trask, the managing editor of a magazine called *Loving More*. The conference Web site says she "has been practicing polyamory for 16 years." But according to the article, "When Trask confronted her husband about sneaking around with a long-distance girlfriend for three months, he denied it. . . . The couple is now separated and plans to divorce." A *Houston Press* article on another couple describes how "John and Brianna opened up their relationship to another woman," but "it ended badly, with the woman throwing dishes." Now they're in another threesome. "I do get jealous at times," John tells the reporter. "But not to the point where I can't flip it off."

Good luck, John. I'm sure polyamorists are right that lots of people "find joy in having close relationships . . . with multiple partners." The average guy would love to bang his neighbor's wife. He just doesn't want his wife banging his neighbor. Fidelity isn't natural, but jealousy is. Hence the one-spouse rule. One isn't the number of people you want to sleep with. It's the number of people you want your spouse to sleep with.

The Bible Doesn't Sanction Polygamy

We've been this way for a long time. Look at the Ten Commandments. One: "Thou shalt have no other gods before me." Two: "Thou shalt not make unto thee any graven image ... Thou shalt not bow down thyself to them, nor serve them: for I the Lord thy God am a jealous God." Three: "Thou shalt not take the name of the Lord thy God in vain." In case the message isn't clear enough, the list proceeds to "Thou shalt not commit adultery" and "shalt not covet thy neighbor's wife."

Some people say the Bible sanctions polygamy. "Abraham, David, Jacob and Solomon were all favored by God and were all polygamists," argues law professor Jonathan Turley. Favored? Look what polygamy did for them. Sarah told Abraham to sleep with her servant. When the servant got pregnant and came to despise Sarah, Sarah kicked her out. Rachel and Leah fought over Jacob, who ended up stripping his eldest son of his birthright for sleeping with Jacob's concubine. David got rid of Bathsheba's husband by ordering troops to betray him in battle. Promiscuity had the first word, but jealousy always had the last.

[Gays are] not looking for the right to sleep around. They already have that. It's called dating.

Gays Want Lasting Relationships

Thousands of years later, we've changed our ideas about slavery, patriarchy, and homosexuality. But we're still jealous. While 21 percent of married or divorced Americans admit to having cheated (and surveys suggest husbands are more likely than wives to stray emotionally and physically), only one in four women says she'd give a cheating husband or boyfriend a second chance, and only 5 to 6 percent of adults consider polygamy or extramarital affairs morally acceptable. As the above cases show, even people who try to practice polygamy struggle with feelings of betrayal.

Krauthammer finds the gay/poly divergence perplexing. "Polygamy was sanctioned, indeed common" for ages, he observes. "What is historically odd is that as gay marriage is gaining acceptance, the resistance to polygamy is much more powerful." But when you factor in jealousy, the oddity disappears. Women shared husbands because they had to. The alternative was poverty. As women gained power, they began to choose what they really wanted. And what they really wanted was the same fidelity that men expected from them.

Gays who seek to marry want the same thing. They're not looking for the right to sleep around. They already have that. It's called dating. A friend once explained to me why gay men have sex on the first date: Nobody says no. Your partner, being of the same sex, is as eager as you are to get it on. But he's also as eager as you are to get it on with somebody else. And if you really like him, you don't want that. You want him all to yourself. That's why marriage, not polygamy, is in your nature, and in our future.

The Government Should Sanction Gay Marriage, Not Domestic Partnerships

Jonathan Rauch

Jonathan Rauch is a senior writer and columnist for National Journal *magazine and a correspondent for* The Atlantic Monthly.

A few days before I began writing this chapter, I sat down to breakfast at a Washington hotel with a prominent conservative writer—a man who, like so many Americans, feels no animus toward homosexuals, indeed wishes them healthy and happy lives, but who is deeply reluctant to tamper with as venerable and important a tradition as marriage. Could we not, he wondered, have the best of both worlds? "Tell me," he said, "why wouldn't civil unions solve this problem?"

For some conservatives, there is no problem to solve. Homosexuals can't marry, and their relationships enjoy no social or legal support. Fine. Their relationships are wicked or trivial, and society has no interest in supporting them; if homosexuals are unhappy, their trouble is their homosexuality, not their marriagelessness. They should become "ex-gays" by praying or getting therapy; or they should repress their sexual desires, pretend to be heterosexual, and fool straight people into marrying them; or they should just go away and stop rocking the boat.

Americans, to their credit, are less and less willing to take such dismissive positions. As more homosexuals come out into the open, more heterosexuals come to realize that homosexuality really exists: that is, there really are people for whom opposite-sex love is not an option, people who nonetheless need love and attachment as much as anybody else. What does society owe such people—and what, for that matter, do they owe society?

Attempts to Deal with Gay Marriage

In the last few years, two quite different answers have emerged, both of them attempts to cope with gay people's marriageless-ness without creating new problems for marriage. One answer might be called privatization, the other substitution—or, as I enjoy calling it, the ABM pact.

Privatizers are primarily libertarians, but they also include a sizable contingent of left-liberals. "Homosexuals have a valid complaint," they say. "It doesn't seem fair to exclude them from civil marriage. But why should there be civil marriage in the first place? Why should the government be in the business of deciding who can marry and who can't? Those judgments rightly belong to individuals. It's not the state's job to privilege one kind of family life over all the others. That is not only unfair, it's unnecessary. If we abolished civil marriage, there would still be lots of marriages. Religious people would marry in their faith and adhere to its marital dictates. Secular people would choose the terms of their own marriage and make a legal contract accordingly. (That sounds like a lot of paperwork, but most people would probably use one of a few standard forms. Anyway, why shouldn't people pay some attention to what they're getting into?) Instead of picking and choosing among relationships, the law would get out of the way. The result would be to make more people happy with their marriages, while sidestepping altogether the looming culture war over state recognition of same-sex unions."

Substituters are not eager to abolish civil marriage; to them, doing so would throw out the baby with the bathwater. "The state has an important role to play in defining and legitimizing marriage," they say. "And the state should steer clear of delegitimizing marriage by redefining it to include same-sex unions. But it is the symbolism of marriage which people are trying to preserve. They don't mind if gay people can put their partners on the company health plan, or if gay people get hospital visitation rights, or if they get inheritance rights. In fact, doing those things seems fair. And aren't such benefits what homosexuals really want and need anyway? Sure, they might prefer a piece of paper from the government, suitable for framing. But nowadays most couples probably can't even find their marriage license. The important thing for gay people is the substance, not the label. So set up 'domestic partnership' programs or 'civil unions' which confer many of the key benefits of marriage. Call the arrangements anything you like—just *don't call them marriage.*"

I call this the ABM pact, for Anything But Marriage. In effect, homosexuals and heterosexuals make a deal. Homosexuals get many of the benefits of marriage, and heterosexuals keep the official designation, with its symbolic and religious baggage. It seems a clever and humane compromise, and indeed it is rapidly becoming the consensus choice in the United States and Europe. Everybody wins, right?

One [approach] sees marriage as a contract between two people. The other sees it as a package of benefits. Well, marriage is indeed both. But it is something much more.

Wrong.

Marriage Involves the Community

Domestic-partner and other marriage-lite arrangements, as I can't resist calling them, do not give homosexuals what they need. They also do not give society what *it* needs. Although not necessarily calamitous, a multitrack system featuring marriage and various forms of pseudomarriage is, at best, a distant second choice to same-sex marriage—not just from homosexuals' point of view but from society's. As for the privatizing approach, it is probably the worst option of all.

The two approaches fail, at bottom, for the same reason: they misapprehend what marriage is. One sees marriage as a contract between two people. The other sees it as a package of benefits. Well, marriage is indeed both. But it is something much more. In the preceding chapter, I sang the praises of marriage's near-magical ability to create kin out of thin air, to turn passion into commitment, to make people healthier and happier, and so forth. From my description, you might assume that I see marriage as some kind of sorcerer's wand: wave it over two people, and their love and lives are transformed.

Would it were so. In fact, as many people know all too well, the marriage vow is not a magical incantation. The weeks and months and then years after the wedding are sometimes harder than the weeks or months or years before. Marriages often fail, sometimes unavoidably. To understand how to preserve the health of marriage as a social institution, and also to understand why there is no substitute for same-sex marriage, it is necessary to understand where marriage gets its special power: how it works. And this depends crucially on understanding that marriage is not merely a contract between two people. It is a contract between two people *and their community*.

For most people, marrying, especially for the first time, is a very big decision. Not for everyone: some people exchange vows in Las Vegas as a lark. But for most, getting married is a life-changing event, one which demarcates the boundary between two major phases of life. Many men and women agonize about marrying. Am I ready? Is he or she the one? And many spouses remember their wedding day vividly for the rest of their lives. People may make many big decisions in life: to join the military, go to graduate school, buy a house, have children, donate a kidney. Yet probably no decision is quite as pregnant with meaning—with the sense of passing across a great divide—as is the decision to marry.

Why should marrying be such a big deal? Partly because the promise being made is extraordinary. That answer, however, begs the question. Why do people take this promise so seriously? The law has made it ever easier for two people to marry, no questions asked, no parental approval needed, no money down. Divorcing is easier, too. Under today's laws, young people could casually marry and divorce every six months as a way of shopping around; but they don't. Most people can expect that marriage will result in parenthood, and parenthood is certainly a momentous thing. Yet even people who, for whatever reason, do not want or cannot have children take marriage seriously. So the questions stand out in sharp relief. Why do we see marrying as one of life's epochal decisions? What gives the institution such mystique, such force?

When two people approach the altar or the bench to marry, they approach not only the presiding official but all of society.

I believe the answer is, in two words, *social expectations*.

Social Expectations Are Important

When two people approach the altar or the bench to marry, they approach not only the presiding official but all of society. They enter into a compact not just with each other but with the world, and that compact says: "We, the two of us, pledge to make a home together, care for one another, and, perhaps, raise children together. In exchange for the caregiving commitment we are making, you, our community, will recognize us not only as individuals but as a bonded pair, a *family* granting us a special autonomy and a special status which only marriage conveys. We, the couple, will support one another.

You, society, will support us. You expect us to be there for each other and will help us meet those expectations. We will do our best, until death do us part."

In every marriage, social expectations are an invisible third partner. Friends, neighbors, parents, and in-laws heap blessings and congratulations on newlyweds, but their joy conveys an implicit injunction: "Be a good husband or wife. We're counting on you." Around the pair is woven a web of expectations that they will spend nights together, socialize together, make a home together—behavior which helps create a bond between them and make them feel responsible for each other. ("It's one A.M. Do you know where your spouse is?" Chances are you do.) Each spouse knows that he or she will get the first phone call when the other is in trouble or in need; and each knows that the expected response is to drop everything and deal with the problem.

Announce to your friends and coworkers that you're getting married, and they say not "That's interesting" or "Best of luck," but "That's wonderful! Congratulations!" Announce it to a parent, and frequently the reaction will be tearful. Stag parties and bridal showers signal that what is beginning is not just a new legal status or a new romantic episode or a new housing arrangement but rather a new stage of life. Expensive gifts deter casual commitment and make bailing out embarrassing. Many of the gifts are household items, appropriate for people about to make a home. The gifts express affection, but each comes with a hidden message: "We expect."

All Weddings Are Public

Then there is the wedding. It is not just a social occasion; it is a whole social technology. A few people (my sister, for one) hold private weddings with, at most, a handful of guests; but even the most private wedding involves not two people but three. Two people cannot marry each other; they must marry before a member of the clergy or a magistrate or clerk—

someone to be the eyes and ears of society. In that sense, all weddings are public. If two people say their vows in the forest, with no one else around, they are not really married at all.

Most weddings, of course, are not just public ceremonies but major events. The most important people in the partners' lives—their families above all—are invited, and many of them come, sometimes traveling across the country or the world. The partners want to affirm their commitment not just in each other's eyes but in the eyes of the people who matter most. Each implicitly says to the other: "All of these people—my family, my friends, and your people, too—have heard my vow. That tells you I meant what I said." Often, though, it is the parents, especially the mothers, who want a really big wedding. The pride they express in their children's matrimony is another subtle—maybe not so subtle—way to say, "We have a stake in this union, too." A hundred witnesses, five hundred, they all heard the couple express their commitment. The presence of the guests, their joy, their smiles and snuffles, stamp the day as a rite of passage. The vows are sealed by the tears of the mothers in the front row: tears which tell the couple and the world, "This promise is important. This promise is like no other."

Marriage is a life-altering boundary. . . . You're on one side or the other. And now you have officially crossed over.

After the wedding come countless smaller gestures of community recognition and community interest. From now on, invitations arrive addressed to two people, not just one. Polite people do not neglect to say, "Give my best to your husband" or "How's the wife?"—casual reminders that, in the world's eyes, you're attached to somebody. If things go badly, expressions of concern and sometimes gossipy chitchat ("Why does she put up with that cheating bastard Frank?") quietly reinforce the community's stake. Anniversary parties bring together friends and family to celebrate that the marriage is intact (no awkward questions asked). The magic of marriage is that it wraps each partnership in a dense web of social expectations, and uses a hundred informal mechanisms to reinforce those expectations.

Marriage Is a Life-Altering Boundary

Law matters, too. I mentioned in the previous chapter that most of the legal benefits and prerogatives of marriage have to do with creating rights of kinship and helping to cope with the burdens of caregiving; and so they do. Individually, each legal provision underscores that the spouses' job is to be there for each other. At least as important, however, is what I think of as the metamessage, which the bundle of legal prerogatives brings. You and your partner can go to a lawyer and arrange many (not all!) of the legal ties of marriage, but by delivering the whole package all at once the government signifies that, after your wedding, you are a different kind of person—a married person. It is not just that you have chosen to assume this or that responsibility. You have bought into the whole deal. "Marriage is a life-altering boundary," the law is saying. "You're on one side or the other. And now you have officially crossed over."

Marriage is coercive, but in the best possible way, which is to say, the softest. The reward for marrying successfully is approval and respect: the penalty for failing in marriage is sympathetic disappointment. The days are over when single people hit a low glass ceiling in business or politics, but married people are still often considered to have greater personal stability and social standing. The days are over, too, when single people were objects of pity or scorn ("Poor thing—she'll be an old maid if she doesn't marry soon"); but when Grandma cluck-clucks over a still-unmarried young man, or when Mom says she wishes her daughter would settle down, she is expressing a preference—one which is echoed in a thousand subtle ways throughout society and which produces a gentle but persistent pressure to form and sustain unions. Marriage is not mandatory, and never should be; but it is *expected*. Getting married is the normal thing for adults to do. More than any other action, institution, or designation, it separates the grownups from the kids. Divorce is not forbidden and never should be; but it is *sad*. Even in an age of common, sometimes nearly instant divorce, every married couple is aware that, in society's eyes, a divorce, even a necessary divorce, is an occasion for commiseration, a kind of failure. When someone says he just went through a divorce, people's first reaction is, "Gosh, I'm sorry," not "Bully for you!" Such are the external prods and lures which create and sustain marriages: soft enough not to be censorious or oppressive, but strong enough to nudge people toward commitment.

Community Begins Where Love Leaves Off

Why the elaborate web of rituals and expectations? Why turn marriage into the Brooklyn Bridge of social engineering? The answer isn't obscure. Committing to the care and comfort of another for life is hard. Some couples can stay in love romantically forever, and good for them. Some people find that devotion and self-abnegation come easy, and they are lucky enough to find partners with the same naturally generous character. Some people have the patience of saints. For most ordinary morals, however, love and altruism aren't always enough. Community begins where love leaves off. Community—our desire not to disappoint our parents and in-laws and friends, our hunger for status, our concern for reputation—can never make marriage easy; but, for many of us, it does make marriage easier. It reminds spouses, during the rough patches, of what they mean to each other, by reminding them of what their marriage means to the people who love them.

That is why it is entirely appropriate that married people enjoy special social standing. They are doing something which is difficult, and they are doing it not only for their own sake and their children's, but for the good of the community. The community owes them a debt.

Not All Queers Want to Marry

Laurel Dykstra

Laurel Dykstra is a Canadian writer and illustrator.

As a queer mom, I am compelled by recent media images of gay and lesbian newlyweds from Massachusetts, San Francisco, Oregon, and other spots around the country. I've downloaded some pictures so my kids can see weddings that aren't heterosexual.

Behind all the joy and excitement, there is something sad about them as well. I detect a sense of "we're finally included"—someone else's decision has made our relationships legitimate.

While I find pictures of beaming couples with bouquets poignant, others see them as cause for outrage. I am stunned at the audacity of those who call their homophobia "family values." I am bewildered by those who fear that what they have (or want) is threatened or sullied if we have it, or if we call our relationships by the same name. In this charged atmosphere, rather than celebrating the recent steps towards gay marriage as a progressive victory, I have been thinking a lot about families: my own family, families in Scripture, and what family might mean as we struggle toward the reign of God, the beloved community.

In the Gospel of Mark, Jesus blesses the children and sends the rich young man away. At the end of these object lessons about status, wealth, and the kingdom, Jesus describes a situation that is hauntingly familiar to many gay men and lesbians, trans-people, and bisexuals. Jesus said, "Truly I tell you, there is no one who has left house, brothers, sisters, mother, father, children, or fields for my sake and for the sake of the good news, who will not receive a hundredfold now in this age—

Laurel Dykstra, "We Are Family," *The Other Side*, vol. 40, no. 4, July 2004, pp. 28–30.

houses, brothers, sisters, mothers, children, and fields with persecutions—and in the age to come, eternal life."

Family is a conspiracy of outsiders and rejects, determined to love ourselves and each other in the face of hatred and violence.

For many, coming out to the good news of who we truly are has meant the painful loss of home and family, a situation which is directly linked to the high homelessness and suicide rates of LGBT youth. But out of love and necessity, those of us who can have built our own families in a host of configurations—lovers, friends, ex-lovers, and children. These families support us in a life of joy and of real persecutions in a homo-hating culture.

Family Is a Conspiracy of Outsiders and Rejects

I wish some of these spokespeople for gay marriage and those who advocate for so called family values knew as much about family as my two-year-old twins, Miriam and Harriet. They know that some families have two mamas or papas, that some have one of each, some have grandparents, some have one parent, and some grownups live alone while others live with friends. In their own family, they include each other, myself ("we grew inna your belly"), their sperm-donor papa, god-mother Cathy, five grandparents, one great-grandmother, numerous aunts and uncles (biological and other), several other godparents, a cousin, and some of the friends who live in community with us. Their circle includes a variety of sexual and gender expressions, some racial diversity, and lots of people with disabilities. The girls know that love and caring are what's important. They also know what those who so enthusiastically endorse marriage for gays or straights seem to neglect: that sometimes people in families need to stop living together.

In the nonheterosexual world where I live, "family" does not mean the constellation of individuals and personalities you were born or adopted into; it means something more. Family is a conspiracy of outsiders and rejects, determined to love ourselves and each other in the face of hatred and violence.

Queer Is Good

I am just old enough and out of the closet long enough to remember when people used to say with a certain lift of the eyebrow, "Oh Sally, she's *family*." Referring to one another as family fell out of use, and in the late eighties and nineties gays, lesbians, bisexuals, and transgendered people began to take back the word "queer." Reclaiming a word that had been used by outsiders to hurt and control us, we used Queer with a capital Q to say, "Yeah, we're Queer and Queer is good. It's good to be different, it's good to resist, it's good to love who we love, and it's good to support one another." In contrast to "gay," which seems to imply that we are all White men, the term is meant to acknowledge important differences like race, gender, and class, while honoring that in our outsider status and our determination to be ourselves, we have some common experiences and goals.

My own disquiet around marriage is rooted in my Queer identity. Marriage is largely a gay assimilationist victory. It says, "See, we're just like you; we blend right in; we'll be good." I fear that this "victory" is a political stopping point that serves to domesticate the most "acceptable" of us by letting us in the club. In the words of gay Brit Peter Tatchell, it is "not liberation but capitulation," and it furthers the oppression of the rest of us. The marriage issue allows us to be divided against one another on the basis of how willing or able we are to conform to heterosexual norms. Are we the marrying kind or the other kind?

Historically marriage was a property contract which controlled a woman's sexual expression for a man's benefit, and children were more chattel than autonomous individuals. However we romanticize and dress that up, it's still pretty creepy. Idealizing the privacy and sanctity of marriage and the nuclear family has allowed for the epidemic of domestic violence and has kept women and children trapped in abusive situations. Why do gay men and lesbians, trans-people and bis, with the history of feminism and sexual politics behind us, seek to join a troubled and unhealthy institution—or worse yet, equate its achievement with liberation?

Families Should Not Be Based on Power

One of the most fascinating and overlooked details in that Mark passage about losing and finding family is that when Jesus names the restored family structure, he omits fathers. While disciples left "house, brothers, sisters, mother, father, children, or fields"; they receive back "houses, brothers, sisters, mothers, children, and fields." Fathers, the head of the household, are notably absent from the second list. Following as it does a teaching about status and economics, this is no accident. This is a whole new kind of family where relationships are not based on power and hierarchy.

Many of the material benefits of marriage like tax breaks and health care are based on the idea that there is a "head" of every household, one individual who represents and is responsible for the other members. This is the very idea that Jesus rejects.

I want Queer acceptance and solidarity.

To benefit materially from marriage, one must have significant privilege already—or have a partner who does. When benefits are combined in same-sex partnerships, it is the already privileged—middle-class, Whites, men—who will benefit most. Through marriage the most privileged of us will obtain the things we all deserve: health care, hospital visits from those we choose. I think gays and lesbians, bis and transpeople, who have experienced discrimination and exclusion, need to look out for the weakest, members of our family, not improve the lot of the best off.

Queer Acceptance and Solidarity

And yes, I think that adults who want to should be allowed to marry legally. I don't begrudge anyone their bouquet, their happiness, or their spousal tax break. but I want much more for myself and the people I love than heterosexual society's token inclusion of some of us. I want Queer acceptance and solidarity.

I want to see, "now, in this age," as Mark puts it, a world where monetary or other social benefits do not influence our choice to enter or leave a relationship. Where covenant and commitment are supported by communities, and Queer youth are safe in home, school, and street. Where we understand that ethical sexuality is not limited to cohabiting, heterosexual monogamy. Where no one is stuck in an abusive relationship. Where all work receives a living wage. In the world I yearn and work for, everyone has health care, as Catholic ethicist Mary Hunt says, "because we have bodies, not because we have a particular partner."

These are simple decent things that all of us deserve, not just those who marry. But these visions will be difficult to achieve, and if we allow ourselves to be separated from each other and our allies—single people, poor people, people of color—it will be even harder.

I've got to jump up and dance whenever I hear the Sister Sledge song, "We are family, I got all my sisters with me. We are family; come on everybody and sing!" To me, it is an anthem for a radical inclusion where the meanest bull dyke, the skankiest drag queen, and the scrawniest trans-man are all sisters and brothers who deserve to be treated with love and respect just because they are. That's the kind of family that I want for my kids.

The Slippery Slope to Polygamy and Group Marriage

Stanley Kurtz

Stanley Kurtz is a fellow at the Hoover Institution at Stanford University in Stanford, California.

After gay marriage, what will become of marriage itself? Will same-sex matrimony extend marriage's stabilizing effects to homosexuals? Will gay marriage undermine family life? A lot is riding on the answers to these questions. But the media's reflexive labeling of doubts about gay marriage as homophobia has made it almost impossible to debate the social effects of this reform. Now with the Supreme Court's ringing affirmation of sexual liberty in *Lawrence v. Texas*, that debate is unavoidable.

Among the likeliest effects of gay marriage is to take us down a slippery slope to legalized polygamy and "polyamory" (group marriage). Marriage will be transformed into a variety of relationship contracts, linking two, three, or more individuals (however weakly and temporarily) in every conceivable combination of male and female. A scare scenario? Hardly. The bottom of this slope is visible from where we stand. Advocacy of legalized polygamy is growing. A network of grassroots organizations seeking legal recognition for group marriage already exists. The cause of legalized group marriage is championed by a powerful faction of family law specialists. Influential legal bodies in both the United States and Canada have presented radical programs of marital reform. Some of these quasi-governmental proposals go so far as to suggest the abolition of marriage. The ideas behind this movement have already achieved surprising influence with a prominent American politician.

None of this is well known. Both the media and public spokesmen for the gay marriage movement treat the issue as an unproblematic advance for civil rights. True, a small number of relatively conservative gay spokesmen do consider the social effects of gay matrimony, insisting that they will be beneficent, that homosexual unions will become more stable. Yet another faction of gay rights advocates actually favors gay marriage as a step toward the abolition of marriage itself. This group agrees that there is a slippery slope, and wants to hasten the slide down.

To consider what comes after gay marriage is not to say that gay marriage itself poses no danger to the institution of marriage. Quite apart from the likelihood that it will usher in legalized polygamy and polyamory, gay marriage will almost certainly weaken the belief that monogamy lies at the heart of marriage. But to see why this is so, we will first need to reconnoiter the slippery slope.

Polygamy Advocates

During the 1996 congressional debate on the Defense of Marriage Act, which affirmed the ability of the states and the federal government to withhold recognition from same-sex marriages, gay marriage advocates were put on the defensive by the polygamy question. If gays had a right to marry, why not polygamists? Andrew Sullivan, one of gay marriage's most intelligent defenders, labeled the question fear-mongering—akin to the discredited belief that interracial marriage would lead to birth defects. "To the best of my knowledge," said Sullivan, "there is no polygamists' rights organization poised to exploit same-sex marriage and return the republic to polygamous abandon." Actually, there are now many such organizations. And their strategy—even their existence—owes much to the movement for gay marriage.

Scoffing at the polygamy prospect as ludicrous has been the strategy of choice for gay marriage advocates. In 2000, following Vermont's enactment of civil unions, Matt Coles, director of the American Civil Liberties Union's Lesbian and Gay Rights Project, said, "I think the idea that there is some kind of slippery slope [to polygamy or group marriage] is silly." As proof, Coles said that America had legalized interracial marriage, while also forcing Utah to ban polygamy before admission to the union. That dichotomy, said Coles, shows that Americans are capable of distinguishing between better and worse proposals for reforming marriage.

Polygamy has historically been treated in the West as an offense against society itself.

Are we? When Tom Green was put on trial in Utah for polygamy in 2001, it played like a dress rehearsal for the coming movement to legalize polygamy. True, Green was convicted for violating what he called Utah's "don't ask, don't tell" policy on polygamy. Pointedly refusing to "hide in the closet," he touted polygamy on the Sally Jessy Raphael, Queen Latifah, Geraldo Rivera, and Jerry Springer shows, and on "Dateline NBC" and "48 Hours." But the Green trial was not just a cable spectacle. It brought out a surprising number of mainstream defenses of polygamy. And most of the defenders went to bat for polygamy by drawing direct comparisons to gay marriage.

Writing in the *Village Voice*, gay leftist Richard Goldstein equated the drive for state-sanctioned polygamy with the movement for gay marriage. The political reluctance of gays to embrace polygamists was understandable, said Goldstein, "but our fates are entwined in fundamental ways." Libertarian Jacob Sullum defended polygamy, along with all other consensual domestic arrangements, in the *Washington Times*. Syndicated liberal columnist Ellen Goodman took up the cause of polygamy with a direct comparison to gay marriage. Steve Chapman, a member of the *Chicago Tribune* editorial board, defended polygamy in the *Tribune* and in *Slate*. The New York

Times published a Week in Review article juxtaposing photos of Tom Green's family with sociobiological arguments about the naturalness of polygamy and promiscuity.

The ACLU's Matt Coles may have derided the idea of a slippery slope from gay marriage to polygamy, but the ACLU itself stepped in to help Tom Green during his trial and declared its support for the repeal of all "laws prohibiting or penalizing the practice of plural marriage." There is of course a difference between repealing such laws and formal state recognition of polygamous marriages. Neither the ACLU nor, say, Ellen Goodman has directly advocated formal state recognition. Yet they give us no reason to suppose that, when the time is ripe, they will not do so. Stephen Clark, the legal director of the Utah ACLU, has said, "Talking to Utah's polygamists is like talking to gays and lesbians who really want the right to live their lives."

All this was in 2001, well before the prospect that legal gay marriage might create the cultural conditions for state-sanctioned polygamy. Can anyone doubt that greater public support will be forthcoming once gay marriage has become a reality? Surely the ACLU will lead the charge.

Societies that permit polygamy tend to reject the idea of marital fidelity—for everyone, polygamists included.

Polygamy Is an Offense Against Society

Why is state-sanctioned polygamy a problem? The deep reason is that it erodes the ethos of monogamous marriage. Despite the divorce revolution, Americans still take it for granted that marriage means monogamy. The ideal of fidelity may be breached in practice, yet adultery is clearly understood as a transgression against marriage. Legal polygamy would jeopardize that understanding, and that is why polygamy has historically been treated in the West as an offense against society itself.

In most non-Western cultures, marriage is not a union of freely choosing individuals, but an alliance of family groups. The emotional relationship between husband and wife is attenuated and subordinated to the economic and political interests of extended kin. But in our world of freely choosing individuals, extended families fall away and love and companionship are the only surviving principles on which families can be built. From [the philosopher and theologian] Thomas Aquinas through Richard Posner [a judge in the U.S. court of Appeals for the Seventh Circuit Court], almost every serious observer has granted the incompatibility between polygamy and Western companionate marriage.

Where polygamy works, it does so because the husband and his wives are emotionally distant. Even then, jealousy is a constant danger, averted only by strict rules of seniority or parity in the husband's economic support of his wives. Polygamy is more about those resources than about sex.

Unlike classic polygamy, which features one man and several women, polyamory comprises a bewildering variety of sexual combinations.

Yet in many polygamous societies, even though only 10 or 15 percent of men may actually have multiple wives, there is a widely held belief that men need multiple women. The result is that polygamists are often promiscuous—just not with their own wives. Anthropologist Philip Kilbride reports a Nigerian survey in which, among urban male polygamists, 44 percent said their most recent sexual partners were women other than their wives. For monogamous, married Nigerian men in urban areas, that figure rose to 67 percent. Even though polygamous marriage is less about sex than security, societies that permit polygamy tend to reject the idea of marital fidelity— for everyone, polygamists included.

Mormon polygamy has always been a complicated and evolving combination of Western mores and classic polygamous patterns. Like Western companionate marriage, Mormon polygamy condemns extramarital sex. Yet historically, like its non-Western counterparts, it de-emphasized romantic love. Even so, jealousy was always a problem. One study puts the rate of 19th-century polygamous divorce at triple the rate for monogamous families. Unlike their forebears, contemporary Mormon polygamists try to combine polygamy with companionate marriage—and have a very tough time of it. We have no definitive figures, but divorce is frequent. Irwin Altman and Joseph Ginat, who've written the most detailed account of today's breakaway Mormon polygamist sects, highlight the special stresses put on families trying to combine modern notions of romantic love with polygamy. Strict religious rules of parity among wives make the effort to create a hybrid traditionalist/modern version of Mormon polygamy at least plausible, if very stressful. But polygamy let loose in modern secular America would destroy our understanding of marital fidelity, while putting nothing viable in its place. And postmodern polygamy is a lot closer than you think.

Group Marriages

America's new, souped-up version of polygamy is called "polyamory." Polyamorists trace their descent from the anti-monogamy movements of the sixties and seventies—everything from hippie communes, to the support groups that grew up around Robert Rimmer's 1966 novel *The Harrad Experiment*, to the cult of Bhagwan Shree Rajneesh. Polyamorists proselytize for "responsible non-monogamy"—open, loving, and stable sexual relationships among more than two people. The modern polyamory movement took off in the mid-nineties—partly because of the growth of the Internet (with its confidentiality), but also in parallel to, and inspired by, the rising gay marriage movement.

Unlike classic polygamy, which features one man and several women, polyamory comprises a bewildering variety of sexual combinations. There are triads of one woman and two men; heterosexual group marriages; groups in which some or all members are bisexual; lesbian groups, and so forth. (For details, see Deborah Anapol's "Polyamory: The New Love Without Limits," one of the movement's authoritative guides, or Google the word polyamory.)

Once monogamy is defined out of marriage, it will be next to impossible to educate a new generation in what it takes to keep companionate marriage intact.

Supposedly, polyamory is not a synonym for promiscuity. In practice, though, there is a continuum between polyamory and "swinging." Swinging couples dally with multiple sexual partners while intentionally avoiding emotional entanglements. Polyamorists, in contrast, try to establish stable emotional ties among a sexually connected group. Although the subcultures of swinging and polyamory are recognizably different, many individuals move freely between them. And since polyamorous group marriages can be sexually closed or open, it's often tough to draw a line between polyamory and swinging. Here, then, is the modern American version of Nigeria's extramarital polygamous promiscuity. Once the principles of monogamous companionate marriage are breached, even for supposedly stable and committed sexual groups, the slide toward full-fledged promiscuity is difficult to halt.

Polyamorists are enthusiastic proponents of same-sex marriage. Obviously, any attempt to restrict marriage to a single man and woman would prevent the legalization of polyamory. After passage of the Defense of Marriage Act in 1996, an article appeared in *Loving More*, the flagship magazine of the polyamory movement, calling for the creation of a polyamorist rights movement modeled on the movement for gay rights.

The piece was published under the pen name Joy Singer, identified as the graduate of a "top ten law school" and a political organizer and public official in California for the previous two decades.

Taking a leaf from the gay marriage movement, Singer suggested starting small. A campaign for hospital visitation rights for polyamorous spouses would be the way to begin. Full marriage and adoption rights would come later. Again using the gay marriage movement as a model, Singer called for careful selection of acceptable public spokesmen (i.e., people from longstanding poly families with children). Singer even published a speech by Iowa state legislator Ed Fallon on behalf of gay marriage, arguing that the goal would be to get a congressman to give exactly the same speech as Fallon, but substituting the word "poly" for "gay" throughout. Try telling polyamorists that the link between gay marriage and group marriage is a mirage.

The flexible, egalitarian, and altogether postmodern polyamorists are more likely to influence the larger society than Mormon polygamists. The polyamorists go after monogamy in a way that resonates with America's secular, post-sixties culture. Yet the fundamental drawback is the same for Mormons and polyamorists alike. Polyamory websites are filled with chatter about jealousy, the problem that will not go away. Inevitably, group marriages based on modern principles of companionate love, without religious rules and restraints, are unstable. Like the short-lived hippie communes, group marriages will be broken on the contradiction between companionate love and group solidarity. And children will pay the price. The harms of state-sanctioned polyamorous marriage would extend well beyond the polyamorists themselves. Once monogamy is defined out of marriage, it will be next to impossible to educate a new generation in what it takes to keep companionate marriage intact. State-sanctioned polyamory would spell the effective end of marriage. And that is precisely what polyamory's new—and surprisingly influential—defenders are aiming for.

A Federal Constitutional Amendment Is Needed to Stop Gay Marriage

Robert H. Bork

Robert H. Bork is a professor at the Ave Maria School of Law in Ann Arbor, Michigan, and the Tad and Diane Taube Distinguished Visiting Fellow at the Hoover Institution in Stanford, California.

Within the next two or three years, the Supreme Court will almost certainly climax a series of state court rulings by creating a national constitutional right to homosexual marriage. The Court's ongoing campaign to normalize homosexuality—creating for homosexuals constitutional rights to special voting status and to engage in sodomy—leaves little doubt that the Court has set its course for a right to marry. This is but one of a series of cultural debacles forced upon us by judges following no law but their own predilections. This one, however, will be nuclear. As an example of judicial incontinence, it will rival *Roe v. Wade*, and will deal a severe and quite possibly fatal blow to two already badly damaged but indispensable institutions—marriage and the rule of law in constitutional interpretation.

The wreckage may be subtler but more widespread even than that. Such a decision would ratify, in the most profound way, the anarchical spirit of extreme personal and group autonomy that is the driving force behind much of our cultural degradation. Call it what you will—moral chaos, relativism, postmodernism—extreme notions of autonomy already suffuse our culture, quite aside from any assistance from the courts. But judicial endorsement, which is taken by much of the public to state a moral as well as a legal truth, makes the anything-goes mentality even harder to resist. The principle undergirding radical autonomy is essentially unconfineable. Thus, Justice Byron White, Senator Rick Santorum [R-VA], and [the public intellectual] William Bennett have all made the point that the rationale for same-sex marriage would equally support group marriage, incest, or any other imaginable sexual arrangement.

Radical Autonomy

That surely is the meaning, insofar as it has a discernible meaning, of the imperialistic "mystery passage" first articulated by three justices in a case upholding the right to abortion and repeated in the majority opinion creating a right to homosexual sodomy:

> [Our] law affords constitutional protection to ... the most intimate and personal choices a person may make in a lifetime, choices central to personal dignity and autonomy, [which] are central to the liberty protected by the Fourteenth Amendment. At the heart of liberty [protected by the Constitution] is the right to define one's own concept of existence, of meaning, of the universe, and of the mystery of human life.

The only real hope of heading off the judicial drive to constitutionalize homosexual marriage is in the adoption of an amendment to the Constitution.

Reading these words, it is hard to know what there is left for legislatures to do, since each individual is now a sovereign nation.

The only real hope of heading off the judicial drive to constitutionalize homosexual marriage is in the adoption of an amendment to the Constitution. The language of the amendment now before Congress is this:

Marriage in the United States shall consist only of the union of a man and a woman. Neither this Constitution nor the constitution of any state shall be construed to require that marital status or the legal incidents thereof be conferred upon unmarried couples or groups.

The amendment is intended primarily to stop activist courts from redefining marriage in any way they see fit, as the Supreme Judicial Court of Massachusetts has recently done. The first sentence, however, also limits legislatures by defining marriage as the people of the United States and of the West have known it.

Many Social Conservatives Oppose the Amendment

Given that the stakes riding on the outcome of the effort to adopt the Federal Marriage Amendment (FMA) are so high, it is surprising that so many social conservatives have expressed opposition. Though these are men for whom I have the highest regard, in this instance I think they are mistaken. Their mistake, it seems to me, derives from a conservative constitutionalism which, though laudable in the past, is now, most unfortunately, obsolete. Walter Bagehot, writing of the English constitution in the nineteenth century, said, "[I]n the full activity of an historical constitution, its subjects repeat phrases true in the time of their fathers, and inculcated by those fathers, but now no longer true." So it is with us. Michael Greve [of the American Enterprise Institute] correctly places the same-sex marriage issue in a wider context: "[T]he broader, more menacing problem is judicial usurpation. . . . [W]hat truly grates is the notion of having [homosexual marriage] dictated by willful, contemptuous judges." Conservative constitutionalism today requires taking back the original Constitution to restore the constitutional order and representative government. If that requires amending the Constitution to recall the judges to their proper function, so be it. There is no other remedy available to save or, more accurately, to restore a republican form of government.

The conservative columnists George F. Will and Charles Krauthammer, however, seem to me to illustrate Bagehot's maxim. Will has written that "amending the Constitution to define marriage as between a man and a woman would be unwise for two reasons. Constitutionalizing social policy is generally a misuse of fundamental law. And it would be especially imprudent to end state responsibility for marriage law at a moment when we require evidence of the sort that can be generated by allowing the states to be laboratories of social policy." To his point about the unwisdom of putting social policy in the Constitution, it is fair to reply that the entire document can be seen as expressing social policy, and certainly parts of the Bill of Rights, such as the guarantee of the free exercise of religion, do exactly that. The real difficulty with Will's position, however, is his notion that the states will be allowed to be laboratories of social policy. They will not; the Supreme Court, as in the case of *Roe*, will simply replace the social policies of all of the states with its own policy.

Defense of Marriage Act

The most likely route to that ruling is the following. A homosexual couple will marry in Massachusetts, move to another state (say, Texas), and claim the status and benefits of marriage there. They will cite the Full Faith and Credit Clause of Article IV of the Constitution, which declares that states must accept the public acts of every other state. Texas will refuse recognition, relying on the federal Defense of Marriage Act (DOMA), passed in reliance on Article IV's further provision that Congress may prescribe the effect of such out-of-state acts. The couple will respond with a challenge to DOMA under the federal Due Process and Equal Protection Clauses. The Supreme Court will then uphold their challenge by finding a federal constitutional right to same-sex marriage that invalidates DOMA. The FMA would prevent this almost-certain outcome. Instead of state-by-state experimentation, we are going to have a uniform rule one way or the other: homosexual marriage everywhere or nowhere. The choice is that stark and judges are forcing us to make it.

The cultural aristocracy—the news media, university faculties, many churches, foundations, television networks, and Hollywood—will continue . . . to propagandize massively and incessantly . . . for the right to marriage.

Charles Krauthammer agrees that "there is not a chance in hell that the Supreme Court will uphold" DOMA. He concludes, nonetheless, that "I would probably vote against the amendment because for me the sanctity of the Constitution trumps everything, even marriage." His point would be well taken if it were not much too late to worry about the sanctity of a document the Supreme Court has been shredding for fifty years. Surely the Court's diktats, which are themselves profoundly unconstitutional, are not sacred. As matters now stand, the "sanctity of the Constitution" is a smoke screen providing cover for judicial activism. Taking action through authentically constitutional means to prevent yet another constitutional travesty shows greater respect for the document than standing by while five of nine justices chisel into the tablets of the law the caprices of the elite class to which they respond. An amendment preventing one instance of judicial depredation would at least represent a democratic choice— indeed a choice by supermajorities, given the requirement of a two-thirds vote in each house of Congress and then ratification by three-quarters of the states.

States Should Experiment with Gay Marriage

There is one other objection expressed by Krauthammer, however: "I would be loath to see some future democratic consensus in favor of gay marriage (were that to come to pass) blocked by such an amendment." That objection could, of course, be made to every provision of the Constitution; each and every one precludes some action by a future democratic consensus. If, for example, a national majority should want to make foreign-born naturalized citizens eligible for the presidency or to abolish jury trials in complex lawsuits, that democratic consensus would be frustrated by the Constitution. Michael Greve suggests a constitutional amendment that would preserve the value of state experimentation while heading off the Supreme Court creation of homosexual marriage:

> The United States Constitution shall not be construed to require the federal government, or any state or territory, to define marriage as anything except the union of one man and one woman.

> The United States Constitution shall not be construed to require any state or territory to give effect to any public act, record, or judicial proceeding respecting a relationship between persons of the same sex that is treated as a marriage under the laws of another state or territory.

This amendment would leave states free to give effect to the acts of other states or not, as they see fit. Greve suggests that state legislatures could control the choice through legislation allowing or forbidding their courts to honor out-of-state homosexual marriages.

States Should Not Experiment

There seem both legal and sociological problems with this proposal. The language leaves out of account what state courts may do with state constitutions. A state supreme court could very well hold—and a number of them certainly will—that its state constitution contains a right to homosexual marriage or, alternatively, that its constitution mandates recognition of such marriages contracted elsewhere. It is not a sufficient answer that the citizenry could respond by amending the state constitution. In many states the amending process is quite difficult and time-consuming; and a state supreme court's ruling will itself affect the balance in the electorate. The cultural aristocracy—the news media, university faculties, many churches, foundations, television networks, and Hollywood—will continue, as they have already been doing, to propagandize massively and incessantly for the normality of homosexuality and the right to marry. It may be doubted that many states will muster supermajorities overruling their courts in the face of this cultural tsunami. There seems no way to guard against state court activism on this issue, which we have already seen in Hawaii, Vermont, and Massachusetts, except by a federal amendment that binds state as well as federal courts.

This issue seems to me so important that a fight against it, whatever the odds, is mandatory.

As seems inevitable in discussions about reining in runaway courts, some have suggested that instead of amending the Constitution, Congress should deny all federal courts jurisdiction to deal with the marriage issue. Congress has power under Article III of the Constitution to make exceptions to the appellate jurisdiction of the Supreme Court and to remove lower court jurisdiction. This proposal, though endorsed by a commentator as sound as [the political scientist] Arnold Beichman, is, as always, a nonstarter, and merely diverts some Congressmen from addressing the problem seriously. If the Supreme Court allowed its jurisdiction over a particular subject to be abolished, which is by no means a certainty, the result would be to leave jurisdiction in the state courts. Article VI provides that "the Judges in every State shall be bound" by the Constitution and laws of the United States, and there is no power in either Congress or the state legislatures to take away that jurisdiction. The result, if Congress acted and the Court acquiesced, would be the same as under the constitutional amendment suggested by Michael Greve, except that state courts could rely upon both the federal and state constitutions to invent, as the courts of Massachusetts and Hawaii have under their state constitutions, a right to same-sex marriage. . . .

Americans Must Fight for This Amendment

Is passing the FMA worth the energy and the political risk for politicians, especially when it may well be a losing battle? Social conservatives, Max Boot notes, have been fighting and losing culture wars for decades. That is obvious, but his recommendation that we acknowledge defeat on the issue of homosexual marriage and move on to other issues is bad advice. This issue seems to me so important that a fight against it, whatever the odds, is mandatory. Abandoning resistance here might nevertheless be seen by some as an intelligent strategy, but that would be true only if there were a more defensible line to fall back to. It is difficult to see what line that might be. The cultural left, including homosexual activists, will keep pressing for more. The BBC, as a foretaste of what is to come, has ordered its staff not to use the words "husband" and "wife," since that might seem to indicate that marriage is preferable to other sexual arrangements. In Canada, a pastor has been charged under a hate speech law for publishing instances of the Bible's disapproval of homosexuality. Church leaders who imagine they can negotiate immunities from laws applying to the rest of the population are almost certainly fooling themselves. Liberal autonomists have little or no respect for religion, except to the extent that some clergy can be recruited to advance their causes in the name of religion. The Catholic Church will be a particular target of attack, as it already has been in California, where the state supreme court ruled that Catholic Charities had to provide prescription contraceptive coverage in its health insurance plan for employees.

Boot's advice to cut and run on this issue thus ignores the fact that there are fewer and fewer places to run to. The autonomous drive toward cultural degradation will not leave us in peace, ever. Boot may be right to predict that Republican support for a marriage amendment would make the party "look 'intolerant' to soccer moms whose views on this subject, as on so many others, will soon be as liberal as elite opinion already is." But if that is true, it means that we will lose all the cultural battles of the future, as the soccer moms trail along behind elite opinion. If Republicans refuse to fight cultural battles on that reasoning, they will look cowardly to conservatives, which could be equally disastrous. It would be better to try to convince the soccer moms, who would not be at all happy if their children and grandchildren cohabited instead of marrying, or "married" persons of the same sex.

Finally, it is worth considering that a vigorous campaign for the FMA could have a salutary effect on the American judiciary. The debates, win or lose, might also lead the public to a more realistic view of the courts. As [the conservative] William F. Buckley, Jr. has written on another occasion, "The public—under the tutelage of its moral and intellectual leaders—is being trained, as regards the Supreme Court of the United States when it is interpreting the Constitution, to accept its rulings as if rendered *ex cathedra*, on questions of faith and morals." Thus, a constitutional amendment "done athwart the will of the Court for the first time in modern history . . . would deliver the Republic from a presumptuous ethical-legal tribunal." "The public," Buckley argues, "needs to experience a release from a subtle thralldom to judicial morality." Quite right. Conservative opinion leaders must recognize that the illegitimacy of the rampant judicial constitutionmaking that is before their eyes changes all the old rules about the place of amendments in our polity. The comfortable shibboleths about a heavy presumption against amending the Constitution no longer have much relevance to the brute facts of our political life. So profound is the departure from a republican form of government that the presumption must now be in favor of amending the Constitution whenever the Court runs wild. Homosexual marriage presents just such an occasion, but if our politicians wait until the Supreme Court has done the inevitable, it will probably be too late for an effective response. Catastrophes ought not to be faced in a spirit of resignation.

Organizations to Contact

The editors have compiled the following list of organizations concerned with the issues debated in this book. The descriptions are derived from materials provided by the organizations. All have publications or information available for interested readers. The list was compiled on the date of publication of the present volume; the information provided here may change. Be aware that many organizations take several weeks or longer to respond to inquiries, so allow as much time as possible.

American Civil Liberties Union (ACLU)
125 Broad Street, 18th Floor, New York, NY   10004
(212) 607-3300 • fax: (212) 607-3318
Web site: www.aclu.org

The ACLU, founded in 1920, is a nonprofit organization of more than 500,000 members and supporters. The organization handles nearly 6,000 court cases annually from its offices in almost every state. The mission of the ACLU is to preserve our constitutional rights and to protect segments of the population that have been denied their rights. The organization offers numerous publications and brochures on lesbian, gay, bisexual, and trangender issues, including the *Too High a Price: The Case Against Restricting Gay Parents* (2006) and an annual report on the *Lesbian Gay Bisexual Transgender and AIDS Project.*

Amnesty International
5 Penn Plaza, 14th Floor, New York, NY   10001
(212) 807-8400 • fax: (212) 463-9193
Email: www.amnestyusa.org
Web site: www.amnestyusa.org

Amnesty International is a worldwide movement of people who campaign for internationally recognized human rights. Its vision is of a world in which every person enjoys all of the human rights enshrined in the Universal Declaration of Human Rights and other international human rights standards. The lack of respect, protection, and promotion of the human rights of lesbian, gay, bisexual and transgender persons is of primary concern to Amnesty International. Each year it publishes a report on its work and its concerns throughout the world. It also publishes numerous individual country reports and briefings.

Exodus International

PO Box 540119, Orlando, FL   32854
(407) 599-6872

Exodus is a nonprofit, interdenominational Christian organization promoting the message of Freedom from homosexuality through the power of Jesus Christ. Since 1976, Exodus has grown to include over 120 local ministries in the USA and Canada. It is also linked with other Exodus world regions outside of North America, totaling over 150 ministries in 17 countries. The organization publishes *Exodus Impact*, a monthly newsletter featuring stories of men and women who have overcome homosexuality, and numerous pamphlets, brochures, DVDs, audio CDs, guides, and workbooks.

Human Rights Campaign

1640 Rhode Island Avenue NW
Washington, DC   20036-3278
(800) 777-4723 • fax: (202) 347-5323
Email: hrc@hrc.org
Web site: http://hrc.org

The Human Rights Campaign (HRC) is America's largest civil rights organization working to achieve gay, lesbian, bisexual and transgender equality. By inspiring and engaging all Americans, HRC strives to end discrimination against GLBT citizens and realize a nation that achieves fundamental fairness and equality for all. HRC publishes *Equality*, which covers a range of topics that affect gay, lesbian, bisexual, and transgender Americans.

Lambda Legal

120 Wall Street, Suite 1500, New York, NY 10005-3904
(212) 809-8585 • fax: (212) 809-0055
Email: legalhelpdesk@lambdalegal.org
Web site: www.lambdalegal.org

Lambda Legal is a national organization committed to achieving full recognition of the civil rights of lesbians, gay men, bisexuals, transgender people and those with HIV through impact litigation, education and public policy work. It pursues high-impact litigation, public education and advocacy on behalf of equality and civil rights for lesbians, gay men, bisexuals, transgender people and people with HIV. The organization publishes *eNews*, a monthly newsletter about groundbreaking litigation, education and public policy work. It also publishes an assortment of booklets; tool kits; brochures; and short material on cases, issues, and campaigns.

Log Cabin Republicans

1901 Pennsylvania Avenue NW, Suite 902
Washington, DC 20006
(202) 347-5306 • fax: (202) 347-5224
Email: membership@logcabin.org
Web site: http://online.logcabin.org

Log Cabin Republicans is the nation's largest organization of Republicans who support fairness, freedom, and equality for gay and lesbian Americans. Log Cabin has state and local chapters nationwide. The organization strives to make the Republican Party more inclusive, particularly on gay and lesbian issues. Working from inside the party—educating other Republicans about gay and lesbian issues—is the most effective way to gain new Republican allies for equality. Log Cabin also exists as a voice for GOP values among members of the gay and lesbian community.

National Association for Research and Therapy of Homosexuality (NARTH)

16633 Ventura Boulevard, Suite 1340

Encino, CA 91436-1801

(818) 789-4440

Web site: www.narth.com

NARTH is a nonprofit, educational organization dedicated to affirming a complementary, male-female model of gender and sexuality. Founded in 1992, the organization is composed of psychiatrists, psychologists, certified social workers, professionals, pastoral counselors, and laymen from a wide variety of backgrounds such as law, religion, and education. NARTH publishes numerous online publications on psychological, medical, and social, political, and ethical issues pertaining to homosexuality. It also offers *NARTH NEWS*, an electronic newsletter on group activities, reports, and new stories related to same-sex attractions, reorientation therapy, and medical issues.

National Stonewall Democrats

1325 Massachusetts Avenue NW, Suite 700

Washington, DC 20005

(202) 625-1382 • fax: (202) 625-1383

Email: stonewalldemocrats.org

Web site: www.stonewalldemocrats.org

The National Stonewall Democrats is a grassroots network connecting lesbian, gay, bisexual, and transgender Democratic activists from across the country. With over ninety chapters in the United States, Stonewall is a force for change within the Democratic Party by sensitizing Democratic candidates and officeholders to the political needs of the gay and lesbian community. The group also promotes the party message of economic justice and social progress to the gay and lesbian community and encourages their participation in Democratic candidate campaigns.

New Hope Ministry

PO Box 10246, San Rafael, CA   94912-0246
(415) 453-6475
Web site: www.newhope123.org

New Hope Ministry is a Christ-centered ministry designed to help people struggling with homosexuality leave their past lifestyle and to fully embrace their true identity in Jesus Christ. The ministry upholds God's standard of righteousness and holiness that declares homosexuality a sin, but also affirms his love and redemptive power are able to bring wholeness and restoration to the entire individual, including his or her sexuality. The ministry offers books, workbooks, booklets, CDs, a monthly newsletter, and many online articles.

Ruth Ellis Center

77 Victor Street, Highland Park, MI   48203
(313) 252-1950 • fax: (313) 865-3372
Email: info@ruthelliscenter.com
Web site: www.ruthelliscenter.com

The Ruth Ellis Center is one of only four social service agencies in the nation dedicated to helping LGBT teens and young adults who are experiencing homelessness. No other agency is specifically set up to help the community's teens and young adults who have been discarded by their families. It will house them, feed them, clothe them, counsel them, help them get on their feet and become independent.

Servicemembers Legal Defense Network (SLDN)

PO Box 65301, Washington, D.C.   20035-5301
(202) 328-3244 • fax: (202) 797-1635
Email: sldn@sldn.org
Web site: www.sldn.org

SLDN is a national, nonprofit legal services, watchdog and policy organization dedicated to ending discrimination against and harassment of military personnel affected by the "Don't Ask, Don't Tell" law banning military service by lesbian, gay, and bisexual persons and related forms of intolerance. It provides free legal counseling to service members with legal issues stemming from or related to the "Don't Ask, Don't Tell" law, the regulations governing military service by HIV+ people, and the regulations addressing military service by transgender persons. SLDN publishes a *Survival Guide*, the most comprehensive resource available for service members, their families, and friends regarding "Don't Ask, Don't Tell" and related forms of discrimination.

Bibliography

Books

John-Manuel Andriote	*Victory Deferred: How AIDS Changed Gay Life in America*, Chicago: University of Chicago Press, 1999.
Harry M. Benshoff and Sean Griffin	*Queer Images: A History of Gay and Lesbian Film in America*, Lanham, Md.: Rowman & Littlefield, 2006.
David Blankenhorn	*The Future of Marriage*, New York: Encounter Books, 2007.
Chandler Burr	*A Separate Creation: The Search for the Biological Origins of Sexual Orientation*, New York: Hyperion, 1996.
Ann H. Coulter	*How to Talk to a Liberal (If You Must): The World According to Ann Coulter*, New York: Crown Forum, 2004.
Louis Crompton	*Homosexuality & Civilization*, Cambridge, Mass.: Belknap Press, 2003.
John D'Emilio	*Lost Prophet: The Life and Times of Bayard Rustin*, New York: Free Press, 2003.
James C. Dobson	*Bringing Up Boys*, Wheaton, Ill.: Tyndale House Publishers, 2001.
Alice Echols	*Shaky Ground: The '60s and Its Aftershocks*, New York: Columbia University Press, 2002.

Byrne R. S. Fone   *Homophobia: A History*, New York: Metropolitan Books, 2000.

David France   *Our Fathers: The Secret Life of the Catholic Church in an Age of Scandal*, New York: Broadway Books, 2004.

Abigail Garner   *Families Like Mine: Children of Gay Parents Tell It Like It Is*, New York: HarperCollins, 2004.

Robert P. George (ed.) and Jean Bethke Elshtain (ed.)   *The Meaning of Marriage: Family, State, Market, and Morals*, Dallas: Spence Publishing, 2006.

Brooke Kroeger   *Passing: When People Can't Be Who They Are*, New York: Public Affairs, 2003.

Beth Loffreda   *Losing Matt Shepard: Life and Politics in the Aftermath of Anti-Gay Murder*, New York: Columbia University Press, 2000.

William J. Mann   *Behind the Screen: How Gays and Lesbians Shaped Hollywood, 1910–1969*, New York: Viking, 2001.

Timothy Patrick McCarthy and John Campbell McMillian   *The Radical Reader: A Documentary History of the American Radical Tradition*, New York: New Press, 2003.

David Moats   *Civil Wars: A Battle for Gay Marriage*, Orlando, Fla.: Harcourt, 2004.

Francis Mark Mondimore	*A Natural History of Homosexuality*, Baltimore: Johns Hopkins University Press, 1996.
Darden Asbury Pyron	*Liberace: An American Boy*, Chicago: University of Chicago Press, 2000.
Jonathan Rauch	*Gay Marriage: Why It Is Good for Gays, Good for Straights, and Good for America*, New York: Times Books, 2004.
Justin Richardson et al.	*And Tango Makes Three*, New York: Simon & Schuster Books for Young Readers, 2005.
Craig A. Rimmerman	*From Identity to Politics: The Lesbian and Gay Movements in the United States*, Philadelphia: Temple University Press, 2001.
Lynn D. Wardle	*Marriage and Same-Sex Unions: A Debate*, Westport, Conn.: Praeger, 2003.
Walter L. Williams	*Gay and Lesbian Rights in the United States: A Documentary History*, Westport, Conn.: Greenwood Press, 2003.
Evan Wolfson	*Why Marriage Matters: America, Equality, and Gay People's Right to Marry*, New York: Simon & Schuster, 2004.

Periodicals

Alison Avery et al. "America's Changing Attitudes Toward Homosexuality, Civil Unions, and Same-Gender Marriage: 1977–2004," *Social Work*, vol. 52, no. 1, January 2007, pp. 71–80.

Thomas Bartlett "Coming Out of the Catholic Closet," *The Chronicle of Higher Education*, vol. 52, no. 16, December 9, 2005.

Joseph Bristow "Remapping the Sites of Modern Gay History: Legal Reform, Medico-Legal Thought, Homosexual Scandal, Erotic Geography," *Journal of British Studies*, vol. 46, no. 1, January 2007, pp. 116–143.

Jay Clarkson "'Everyday Joe' versus 'Pissy, Bitchy, Queens': Gay Masculinity on StraightActing.com," *The Journal of Men's Studies*, vol. 14, no. 2, Spring 2006, pp. 191–208.

Midge Decter "Stop Compromising on 'Civil Unions,'" *USA Today* (Magazine), March 2007, pp. 52–54.

Wendy Harris "Out of the Corporate Closet: How African American Gays and Lesbians Can Gain Ground in the Workplace," *Black Enterprise*, vol. 37, no. 10, May 2007, pp. 64–66.

Anissa Helie "Holy Hatred," *Reproductive Health Matters*, vol. 12, no. 23, May 2004, pp. 120–125.

William Stacy Johnson — "A Way Forward? Changing the Conversation on Homosexuality," *The Christian Century*, vol. 124, no. 7, April 3, 2007, pp. 28–34.

Robert Li Kitts — "Gay Adolescents and Suicide: Understanding the Association," *Adolescence*, vol. 40, no. 159, fall 2005, pp. 621–629.

Paul J. Levesque — "Classroom Controversy: Christianity and Gay Rights," *Academic Exchange Quarterly*, vol. 8, no. 2, summer 2004, pp. 259–264.

Brian Lewis — "The Queer Life and Afterlife of Roger Casement," *Journal of the History of Sexuality*, vol. 14, no. 4, October 2005, pp. 363–383.

Rod Liddle — "I Am Sorry, but the C of E Really Must Make Up Its Mind About Homosexuality," *Spectator*, April 14, 2007.

Craig M. Loftin — "Unacceptable Mannerisms: Gender Anxieties, Homosexual Activism, and Swish in the United States, 1945–1965," *Journal of Social History*, vol. 40, no. 3, spring 2007, pp. 577–597.

Michael Lombardi-Nash — "1904: The First Lesbian Feminist Speaks," *The Gay & Lesbian Review Worldwide*, vol. 11, no. 3, May–June 2004, pp. 31–35.

Martin F. Manalansan   "Queer Intersections: Sexuality and Gender in Migration Studies," *International Migration Review*, vol. 40, no. 1, spring 2006, pp. 224–250.

Maria Morris   "Queer Life and School Culture: Troubling Genders," *Multicultural Education*, vol. 12, no. 3, spring 2005.

Richard John Neuhaus   "Homosexual but No Longer Gay," *First Things*, vol. 166, October 2006, pp. 69–71.

David A. Niose   "Humanism and the Gay Community," *The Humanist*, vol. 66, no. 3, May–June 2006, p. 45.

Matthew Parris   "Why Is It So Hard for Christian 'Moderates' to Defend Their Views with Passion," *Spectator*, November 18, 2006.

James A. Sanders   "Jesus, the Bible, and Homosexuality: Explode the Myths, Heal the Church," *Biblical Theology Bulletin*, vol. 37, no. 1, spring 2007, pp. 41–42.

Theo G. M. Sandfort   "Sexual Orientation and Gender: Stereotypes and Beyond," *Archives of Sexual Behavior*, vol. 34, no. 6, December 2005, pp. 595–612.

Anne Stockwell   "All of Me: In the NBA John Amaechi Didn't Lie. He Just Didn't Say He Was Gay," *The Advocate*, March 13, 2007, pp. 42–50.

Mariana Valverde "A New Entity in the History of Sexuality: The Respectable Same-Sex Couple," *Feminist Studies*, vol. 32, no. 1, spring 2006, pp. 155–163.

Cynthia G. Wagner "Homosexual Relationships: Institutional Support Might Bring More-Stable Relationships Among Gays," *The Futurist*, vol. 40, no. 3, May–June 2006, p. 6.

Index

225

W

Wakefield, Tim, 114
Wall Street Journal, 30
Warner, Michael, 152
War on Terror, 109
Washington Blade, 78
Weddings
    public aspect of, 182–184
    traditional vs. same-sex, 187
Wertham, Fredric, 26–28
Werthheim, L. Jon, 111–114
What is Marriage For? The Strange Social History of Our Most Intimate Institution (Graff), 165–166
What's the Matter with Kansas? How Conservatives Won the Heart of America (Frank), 89
While Europe Slept: How Radical Islam is Destroying the West from Within (Bawer), 79

White, Byron, 203
Wilcox, Clyde, 132–140
Will, George F, 205
Will & Grace (television show), 112
Williams, Rowan, 116
"The Windsor Report," 116
Withers, Kristine, 77–78
Wolfson, Evan, 164–172
Women
    solicitation of males by, 50
    portrayal of, as villainesses 27–28
Workshops, GLSEN-sponsored, 153
Worthen, Frank, 60–61

Z

Zero tolerance policy, of Vatican, 147–148
Zorn, Eric, 169–170, 171